In *Relationships over Rules*, David reminds us that where you come from does not dictate who you are or where you can go. Knowing David personally, he walks the walk, helping people of all paths of life. This book will not only encourage you to reach your true potential, but it will also show you how to push past what the world says is possible.

Mark Robinson, lieutenant governor, North Carolina

Our world is so focused on the next sale, the next transaction, and even the next relationship, but David's story of resilience and achievement reveals that God has already equipped us with everything we need: the people already in our lives. His real-life examples, wise principles, and practical tools will empower you to overcome adversity, invest in those around you, and fulfill God's plan for your life—your true potential.

David and Jason Benham, best-selling authors,
TV and podcast hosts, and entrepreneurs

David's book, *Relationships over Rules*, is a great reminder that putting value in relationships will carry you much further than our society tends to indicate. His personal story is a shining example of this, and as a friend of David's for many years, I can confidently say that his success is directly tied to his relational equity.

Landon Cassill, NASCAR driver

Why do so many people feel more alone than ever before? Fear, social media, and the instant-gratification culture have made it easy to devalue personal connections, patience, and focus. *Relationships over Rules* shows how these very concepts are the antidote for the modern condition, offering a framework that's easy to understand, implement, and maintain in your everyday life. David's journey to find his place in family, business, and community is a wonderful story of adversity, self-discovery, passion, and perspective. *Relationships over Rules* is a joy to read!

Rick Oppedisano, founder and CEO, Delta Bravo

Not all of you reading this book have had the privilege of knowing David personally, but by the time you turn the last page, you will want to, and to some extent, due to his great storytelling ability, you might think you do know him. As I read *Relationships over Rules*, I felt like we were grabbing a cup of coffee, catching up on life and business like we try to do every few months. David beautifully weaves his personal journey of life with timeless life principles and a few original tricks of the trade that have made him into the successful kingdom-minded man, husband, and father he is today.

Josh Blackson, COO and pastor, Elevation Church

I've seen David Hoffman's words in practice. He was my friend for eight years before I became his real estate client.

As a well-served client and a well-nurtured friend, I have witnessed David living out the principles for relational success he explains in *Relationships over Rules.* You don't want to miss the compelling story of his difficult youth or the intensity of purpose and insight that grew out of it and into the light of Jesus Christ.

Dan Bishop, congressman, North Carolina

Relationships over Rules offers an inspiring perspective on David's journey of creating a successful real estate company. The timeless wisdom shared in this book is invaluable!

Chris Manhertz, tight end, #84, Jacksonville Jaguars

If the idea of purposeful friendship, the power of being present, and maximized relationships that create win-win outcomes intrigues you, then this book will blow you away. David's masterful creativity in weaving his and Jessica's inspirational story as a backdrop for developing a Christ-centered framework for decision-making makes this book a must-read. This book is so timely and will keep you turning through the wonderful pages to uncover nuggets of truths to guide you in your quest of pursuing success God's way.

Dr. Manny Ohonme, founder, president, and CEO,
Samaritan's Feet International

I have known David Hoffman for years. I have always found his life story compelling and encouraging. As David shares his story in this book, he lists the principles by which he has chosen to live. I've always believed and taught that when confronted with a decision, if you can't apply one of your chosen life principles, don't make the decision. David knows well his chosen life principles. He consistently lives by them, and the subsequent success in his life is obvious. I hope the readers of this book make many of these principles their own. If so, they will be stronger and better in life as they do.

David Chadwick, founder and senior pastor,
Moments of Hope Church

There is no better time than now to highlight the significance of putting relationships above all else. In *Relationships over Rules*, David demonstrates how intentionally serving others both personally and professionally will set you on a path filled with purpose. The principles that have guided David throughout his life can be modeled and put into action by every person who is fortunate enough to read this book. David's words will inspire us to focus on adding value to those around us on a consistent basis. I hope the wisdom in this book encourages all of us to make relationships the leading rule.

Michael Brennan, president, Movement Mortgage

Relationships over Rules

7 Principles to Lead Gracefully and Love Generously

DAVID HOFFMAN

with Robert Noland

BroadStreet
PUBLISHING

BroadStreet Publishing® Group, LLC
Savage, Minnesota, USA
BroadStreetPublishing.com

Relationships over Rules: 7 Principles to Lead Gracefully and Love Generously

9781424566648 (hardcover)
9781424566655 (ebook)

Stock or custom editions of BroadStreet Publishing titles may be purchased in bulk for educational, business, ministry, fundraising, or sales promotional use. For information, please email orders@broadstreetpublishing.com.

Published in association with the literary agency of WTA Media, LLC, Franklin, Tennessee.

Cover and interior by Garborg Design Works | garborgdesign.com

Printed in China

23 24 25 26 27 5 4 3 2 1

To Mom—

For your selfless sacrifice to bring me into the world, for being my lifelong role model of gratitude and faithfulness, for giving me the motivation that drives my purpose, each and every day.

To Jessica, Kane, and Knox—

I would not have the courage to share these stories and principles with the world if it were not for my best friend and bride, Jessica, who loves and fears the Lord immensely and whom I met the day after becoming a Christian. Jessica has been by my side through deep valleys and tall peaks. I hope and trust that our boys, Kane and Knox, will follow Jesus for all of their days on this earth and embrace Jessica's passion for the Word, which honors Proverbs 22:6, ensuring for them this truth that they will spend eternity in heaven.

Our Savior Jesus poured out new life so generously.
God's gift has restored our relationship with him and given us back our lives. And there's more life to come—an eternity of life! You can count on this.

Titus 3:3–8 MSG

CONTENTS

MY STORY

My mom was beautiful. Beautiful inside and out. She appeared to be the picture of health. But at just seventeen years old, she was diagnosed with multiple sclerosis (MS). Today, with the many medical developments and treatments available, people have an opportunity to effectively manage MS. For some, you may never know that they have such a horrible disease. But this was many years ago. My mom's life was forever changed.

Three years after she married my dad, while in her late twenties, she became pregnant. Bottom line—in those days, doctors advised women with MS not to have babies. Yet despite their stern warnings of what could happen to her because of the pregnancy, particularly in the trauma of birth, my mom chose to take the risk and carry me.

Her plight would become a reflection of my own life because I seemed to be in a constant battle for survival until I became a young man. Living versus dying. Risk versus reward. Rules versus relationships. I experienced the good in this world from my mother and the evil that works to rob, kill, and destroy by the hand of others. But that is what made and molded me into who I am today. I learned fast that adversity can create gratitude if you just allow it to.

From my story came my life's principles, the foundation I have laid upon which to build my businesses and a life blessed beyond measure. I hope and pray that you find yourself in these pages and that, when you do, the power of your own relationships will connect like never before.

1

GOD MUST BE A METS FAN

In November of 1979, my time had come to enter the world. Just as the doctors had warned, after I was born, my mom fell into a brief coma. But after returning to consciousness, she appeared to be fine. With me being perfectly healthy, we were soon released to go home.

Eight months later, in some sort of delayed trauma from the pregnancy and delivery, Mom's condition accelerated, and she became paralyzed from the waist down. When I was barely two years old, my dad made the horrible decision to leave her and take me with him. His selfish choice triggered a tragic trajectory in my life. Separating any child from a loving and nurturing mother is devastating to both. But that's exactly what happened to me.

Four to five times a year, not nearly enough, my dad arranged for me to go visit my mom. Our family had lived in Brooklyn, but Mom moved to a small apartment in Staten Island where the cost of living was cheaper. Dad and I lived in Queens. I couldn't appreciate it at the time, but looking back, Mom had this incredible panoramic view of the Statue of Liberty. Her windows acted as a frame around a beautiful landscape canvas of Lady Liberty. Whether in the daytime against the backdrop of a blue sky or at night with the lights showcasing her in the harbor, the view was stunning. Always present, eternally optimistic, and a beacon of hope—just like my mother.

Because my dad left her with no income, Mom applied for Medicaid and got professional services that came in several times a week. (Years later, Dad would offer me this as his reason for leaving: without his income, Mom could qualify for government assistance to receive the level of care she required.)

Because she could no longer walk, Mom was confined to a wheelchair. But everything else about her was full of life. Her mind was sharp, and her heart was full. Any time I spent with her was amazing and always over far too soon. I *never* wanted to leave. At least when she was with me, Mom kept the biggest smile on her face. I can't say it enough—beautiful inside and out.

Every time I would go visit her, I remember thinking, *Why am I not* here? *With* her? *She clearly loves me. My heart is here with my mom.* I was older before I began to have thoughts and questions like, *What kind of a man leaves his wife in this condition?* If anyone in our family had a right to be bitter, it was my mom, but she *never* was.

When I was five years old, Dad remarried. After what felt like overnight to me, I had a stepmother. As can happen with children in second marriages, I came to see that this woman wanted a husband but *not* a stepson. Before I knew it, my life began to change from bad to worse.

Moses versus Mary

My mom was raised Catholic, but because my father was Jewish, she had made the difficult decision to convert to Judaism. Now alone and abandoned, Mom returned to her roots, clinging tightly to her faith in God to help her survive a broken home and a broken heart from the confines of her wheelchair. But now free to express her faith, she had a Bible and small statues of Jesus displayed proudly in her living room.

When I went to go visit Mom, she was always beaming. When I heard her on the phone, she was always laughing as she talked. I made the connection between my mom's unexplainable joy amid such terrible circumstances to the very little I knew of the Jesus she talked about—who loved others even though he was ultimately betrayed.

Over all those years, I never heard my mom say a bad word about my father. Or about my stepmother. Or about anyone for that matter. As I got older, I began to think, *I don't love the people I live with, and they obviously don't love me, but if my mom can stay positive on this road she's been forced to go down, then I can do it too.* Mom's faith was having a very slow and subtle effect on me, like grains of sand sifting one at a time inside an hourglass.

The woman my dad married was Jewish like him. This further reinforced the strictness of how I was raised in their religion. From my earliest memories, their belief system was all Jehovah, no Jesus. No Holy Spirit. And completely unlike the Trinity, no love.

Like any boy born into a devout and dedicated Jewish family, I had to memorize the Torah—the first five books of the Bible. (This discipline at such an early age certainly helps develop a young brain.) Attending my weekly class at the temple, I remember sitting there contemplating, *I'm going to be a man. This is a big deal.* I accepted this as something I had to do. But I have always been really good at rule following.

I liken my memorization of the Torah to giving me an eighty-thousand-word Russian novel and telling me that, in a year, I had to have it memorized. So I learned the text by rote but had no idea what it was actually talking about and certainly, as a child, no idea how it applied to my life. Because I had no real foundation in faith, the Book to me was just historical literature that I had to be ready to regurgitate. There were no "whys" behind the "whats." Yet, through constant repetition, I took in the text so I could do well when I was tested. I did whatever my stepmother and father told me to do—literally—to the letter of the law. I always desperately wanted to be obedient, so I adhered to the code even with no context. I didn't buck the system. Memorized without meaning. Went through the motions with no emotion. That was my life as a kid. That's how I survived.

As many know, in Judaism you can't write out the word *God*. In the Jewish heritage, out of a holy awe or fear, you have to leave out a letter, usually the *o*. We celebrated Hanukkah in December. Passover in April. No Christmas. When people ask me how I was able to ignore Christmas as a kid when the entire world was celebrating, the best way I can explain the mindset is that it's like driving down the highway in a lot of traffic. You just focus on what's in front of you. Where *you're* going. You don't really even notice the other cars passing by. I just didn't think twice about what Christmas was or why others celebrated the holiday and we didn't. Believe it or not, I was in my thirties before I even realized the name of Christ is the root word in Christmas.

Starting at around the age of eight, I would fast on Yom Kippur. For twenty-four hours, I had no food and nothing to drink. I wouldn't even brush my teeth because I avoided water. I'd wake up on that day each year and walk down to the convenience store to get my stepmom and sister their bacon-egg-and-cheese sandwiches. I can distinctly recall being asked one time to also pick up barbecue potato chips and Hershey chocolate bars. I would go pick up their food, deliver it all to the table, and retreat to my room. A vivid memory, like it was yesterday.

Proven by that example, my family's adherence to being a strict Jewish household was certainly far more by word than deed because I was the only one who held to the traditions on holy days. What I was being taught at the temple, I obeyed. But if I dared ask my stepmom why they didn't take part, I would be told, "Shut your mouth," or "Just be happy someone wants you," or "Be glad you have somewhere to live."

Like the Christmas question, when asked why I worked so hard to adhere to the traditions when my family didn't and wouldn't, my only answer is that I have always had this deep, innate sense of the law, right and wrong, black and white. When I was told that I needed to repent on this one day of the year and "suffer," I was well aware that I wasn't perfect like God, so I felt I needed to obey. That compliance was just another step in always working hard for approval through my behavior. I wanted to avoid the commission of the wrong things *and* the omission of the right things. While my life exemplified no faith, a constant burden of works was growing heavier in my heart.

Over the years growing up in a Jewish community, we attended other families' bar mitzvahs in our area of New York City. When my own took place, our rabbi tested me. As a kid, and fitting with my personality to this day, I was 100 percent all in. Rules. Standards. A rigid structure. I was good at it. I worked hard to comply. And I passed with flying colors.

If a box was *supposed* to be checked, I *had* to check it.

Dehydration, Starvation, and Isolation

But because of how detached my family was from any sort of lifestyle reflecting faith and because my stepmother was fully in control of the family, more and more rules were placed on me until their house became a prison with a sentence of solitary confinement.

In 1987, my dad and stepmom had my half sister. Her nursery was right next to my bedroom. When I was not at school, I had to stay in my room. Going out my door without permission meant severe punishment. As my sister became a toddler, knowing she had a playmate in the bedroom next door, she wanted to crawl over into my room, but she wasn't allowed. She would come up to the threshold and stop as she was trained to do. Yet somehow, even with the limitations, we managed to forge a strong sibling connection. Probably because of loneliness.

There's one major problem when you are confined to your bedroom as a child: no water and no food. The only time I could get a drink or eat was if they chose to bring something to me or allowed me out for a few minutes. The times they brought me anything became less and less frequent. At school, I had to make sure I drank as much water as I could to hold off the thirst for as long as possible when

I got home. That, of course, made the weekends really long and very hard to endure.

When I would request something to eat or drink or work up the courage to ask my stepmom why I couldn't come out of my room, she would just scream at me and make threats. As a child in that kind of dictatorial environment, you eventually stop asking and just accept that you are a servant to a master. Oddly, my stepmom never hit me. At least not physically. But there were times when I believe I would have traded a beating for a taste of normal childhood freedom. Their address became the house where I survived, but it was *never* my home.

Poverty for my family was not the issue. I knew my parents went to the store regularly and had plenty of food in the kitchen. And, like I said, they often sent me to the store to get their food, then carefully scrutinized the receipt and the change to be sure that I hadn't bought anything else. I only got what they chose to give me. They never allowed me to eat "their food." If they had cookies, my stepmom would keep count of them. If one was "missing," even if someone else had eaten it, she blamed and punished me.

For lunch at school, my stepmom always made me a bologna sandwich—one slice of whatever substance that was on two pieces of white bread. On a generous day I might find a dot of mustard. I was given the old bread, so it was crusted around the edges and would often have the little green circles of mold. On the way to school, I would check the bread and peel them off so no one would see what I was having to eat. My friends would often notice the difference between their lunches and mine and share some of their food. Anytime a teacher would try to raise a question to my stepmother about my lunch at school (or lack thereof), my stepmother was always adamant, offering plausible reasons why I was only allowed to eat what she provided. Somehow, she always managed to keep anyone from intervening to help me.

Our next-door neighbor ran a bakery and had picked up on how I was treated. He started sneaking me sacks of bread when I got home from school. I would hide behind the garage and eat the fresh baguettes he gave me before going in the house. One time, my stepmom's sister and her husband confronted my parents about their treatment of me and threatened to call the police. My stepmom shut her down, and they stopped talking. But that was all I knew and all I could remember, so I didn't realize how bad my circumstances actually were as a kid. Especially in grade school, I just thought it was how *my* life was.

Once when my dad was at work and my stepmom went out for the evening, she got a sitter. Of course, the girl was told I had to stay in my room. But I saw a window of opportunity. I ran the water in the bathtub so I could drink it, figuring she would just think I was getting ready for bed. When my stepmom returned, she asked the sitter if I had done anything. The girl responded, "No, he just took a bath." She had no idea that her answer of me running water without permission meant punishment.

But I finally realized I had access to water twenty-four seven, anytime I wanted—in the toilet. There was always water down in the bowl, and the sound of a flush brought no suspicion. Relieving myself was about the only thing I didn't have to ask permission to do, and the water in the commode wasn't measured. So, unbeknownst to my dad and stepmom, the toilet solved my thirst problem.

Constant hunger causes someone to get desperate as well as creative. My parents had a dog, and they stored his food down in the basement. My stepmom never kept track of it, so I started sneaking down there at night to eat from the bag. I could never say, "They treated me like a dog," because they actually took better care of their pet than they did of me.

From the Frying Pan into the Fire

When I was eleven years old, one day, out of nowhere, my dad left. Like, for good. This time, he left me too. Now, it was just me and my half sister with my stepmom. With my dad gone and as I got older, I fought harder to call and visit my mother. I would work to find ways to go see her. A constant question rolling around in my heart and mind was *Why can't I live with my mother, the one person who I know loves me?* A dear friend, mentor, and pastor often says that the most heard word in heaven will be *oh* as we learn why things happened to us here on earth.

Nothing about my life made sense to me at the time.

When I would muster the strength to ask to go live with my mother, my stepmom would answer with cuts like, "I was the only one who protected you. You can go live with your father, but *neither* of your parents wants you. That's why you don't live with your mom and why he left you with me. In fact, David, *no one* wants you." And her worst verbal jab was "Your mom didn't know she was going to get sick when she had you. If she did, she would have aborted you."

The few times a year I was able to be with my mom, she would tell me that her God in heaven was also a Father. Because I respected her so much, I believed her. But then that meant that he allowed me to be taken away from her and sent to live with a dad and stepmom who made my life a living hell. While she told me that God loved me, my circumstances made that very hard to swallow, so my response was *Well, if that's love, then I hate him.* And of course, as I explained earlier, all this was festering in my heart while I was continuing to strictly follow the laws of Judaism.

I can remember talking to God, saying, *I can't really wrap my mind around why you made my mom so sick and took me away from her. You broke up their marriage and you put me here. Probably because there's seven billion other people you're focused on.* Then, as a boy who loved sports, particularly baseball, I came up with the best diss I could imagine at the time: *God, you know I'm a Yankees fan. You are obviously a Mets fan. So we'll just agree to disagree.* While I was speaking with brutal honesty to the Almighty, like King David always did, I wasn't exactly writing psalms.

Because I started school early as a child, I was going to be sixteen in my senior year of high school, graduating in 1997. But just as I was about to start back in the fall of 1996, my stepmom met a man who lived in northern Virginia. She made the decision that we would move there, closer to him. The only good thing was that this guy had a positive effect on her, and she began to soften some. She even came to me once and offered a quasi-apology. I remember her saying, "David, I know I didn't give you the childhood that you deserved. And I know I was hard on you." Regardless of how it came, I was just grateful that there was *any* sort of change for the better.

As an adult, when I began to deal with my past and try to reconcile my upbringing, I actually came to lay more of the responsibility for the abuse at my father's feet. I liken what happened in their house to Adam and Eve in the garden. Did Eve listen to the serpent and give in to sin? Yes. But Adam was the one whom God placed there first and made the leader. He could have intervened and changed the outcome. But when the crisis came, he just chose not to. So it was with my situation. My dad could have ended the way I was treated anytime. But just like Adam, he chose not to do anything. Until he left, for good.

Independence Day

Fast-forward to my sister's sixteenth birthday party. By that time, I was in my early twenties and out on my own. For the past several years, as my stepmom had been able to have a much happier life with her new husband, she was much nicer to me, and we got along better. But the root of the original conflict between her and me was still always there. Now, being older, more mature, and a little wiser, on this particular visit to my stepmom's house, I finally saw the light.

I had brought a date with me, arriving early for my sister's party. My date and I had gotten into a friendly debate on some current topic. Finally, I said, "Okay, let's look it up online." I asked my stepmom, as I had always been trained to do, "Can we look it up on your computer?"

She responded, "Well, the computer doesn't work."

As our little discussion continued, my stepmom began to join in. Suddenly, without thinking, she jumped up, went over to the computer, and got online. When she wanted to use it, everything was working fine. I took note but moved on.

I had brought some food with us and asked if we could use the microwave to warm it up. Once again, her answer was "No, it's not working." That's when I had officially had enough. Finally speaking my mind, I stated, "Wait a minute. I think the issue actually is that *I'm* just not allowed to touch *anything. I'm* not allowed to use *anything* of yours. That's the real truth here."

We've all heard the stories of people of any age who are held captive for so long that they just give up and give in to their fate. We can hear those people talk about the times they had opportunities to escape and didn't. That's when we on the outside usually respond, "What! Why didn't you run? Why didn't you take the opportunity to get out? Are you crazy? That's what I would have done." But here's the problem: it *wasn't* you. None of us knows, when our minds are trained and brainwashed, how we will respond to that level of manipulation and psychological control. I can tell you firsthand, especially as a kid, when you don't know what to do, it's just so easy to not do *anything* but comply.

But this time, in a sudden flash of revelation and raw courage, something connected in me. There was a shift in my heart. I realized I just couldn't do it anymore. I wasn't going to take it. I took my date by the hand and walked out. For the last time.

I finally opened the cell door and set myself free from *everyone* who had hurt me. Time to live life fully on *my* terms. By now, I wanted nothing to do with the God of *anyone's* belief system. After all, the Almighty might be for the Mets, but *I* was a New York Yankees fan.

2

NOTHING IS CERTAIN BUT DEATH AND TAXES

My entrepreneurial leanings started early out of necessity. Trying to survive as a kid and wanting my own money for anything I needed, by the age of eight all the way up into high school, I learned the power of supply and demand. Maintaining high profit with a low overhead. I washed cars in the spring. I mowed lawns in the summer. I raked leaves in the fall. I shoveled snow in the winter. Thank God for four distinct seasons in New York, where each created a market opportunity on which I could capitalize. I'm grateful that, early on, I developed a strong work ethic that has always served me well, regardless of the motivating factors.

Now out on my own in my late teens, I desperately wanted to make the most of my life. For me, that meant furthering my education. I wanted to go to college. But, as you might suspect, I had no extra money left over each month after paying my bills. Enrolling in the local community college, I juggled three jobs around my class schedule. Being a waiter, or a server as it's known today, was my primary go-to. The tips made my punches count during the evening and weekend shifts.

In 2001, at twenty-one years old, I was in my senior year at George Mason University in Fairfax, Virginia, closing in on an economics degree. One day in the hallway between classes, one of my professors, Mark Crain, walked up to me and said, "David, I have an opportunity for you—"

I abruptly interrupted him: "Yes!"

His eyes widened as a look of surprise came across his distinguished face.

Now, let's hit the pause button. Freeze-frame this scene and allow me to explain.

I had been told no all my life. Most of the time aggressively with an exclamation mark. The answer to 99 percent of the questions I asked as a kid were met with various forms of not simply no but "not on your life." Often, some sort of "And here's the reason you don't deserve what you're asking for" was connected. I had been screamed at, yelled at, berated, humiliated, and threatened with constant "you can'ts," "you won'ts," and "you never wills" from my earliest memories. So, now as an independent adult, I was officially done with nos. I was finished with rejections, refusals, and rebuffs.

My life was all about creating as much yes as possible, *for* me and *from* me to others. I didn't just want to hear it; I also wanted to say it! So when a man I respected said my name connected to the words "opportunity for you," that was all I needed to hear. No details. No explanations. No "let me think about it." Just yes. Y-E-S.

Okay, unpause.

Professor Crain gathered his thoughts and continued, ignoring my goofy grin and wild eyes. "There's an opportunity for you to be an economist at the Tax Foundation. I'd like to set up an interview for you."

I had already given him my answer, so I told him to just let me know the day and time and I was *so* there. But then what he was offering me suddenly sank into my heart, and I added a question: "Sir, can I ask…why *me*?"

Professor Crain answered without hesitation, "David, you always ask powerful questions—either ones that haven't been asked yet, those that further the conversation, or both. That, plus it is obvious that you pay attention and are always present."

Here's some context for you: The Tax Foundation was founded in 1937 and, eighty-plus years later, is the nation's leading independent, nonprofit agency on tax policy. Their stated goal is "to improve lives through tax policies that lead to greater economic growth and opportunity" using "principled research, insightful analysis, and engaged experts."[1] *Boom!*

Never Forget

My interview was set up for September 12, 2001, in Washington, DC. *Yes, the day after 9/11 in our nation's capital.*

On the afternoon of the day our entire country was reeling in shock and disbelief, the chief economist at the Tax Foundation called me.

"Hey, David, I wanted to touch base with you about tomorrow."

Without hesitation, I responded, "Yes, we have a meeting tomorrow morning."

He continued, "Yes…but in light of today's events, I wanted to—"

I interrupted his efforts at being sensitive to me and said, "Well, I'll be there unless you were calling to cancel."

A bit surprised, he asked, "So, you're still going to come?"

While I, of course, had no intention of being inconsiderate or disrespectful to anyone, especially in light of what had happened on this horrible day, I felt even more determined to say yes and press on into the future that those terrorists had every intention of stopping for us all. I refused to be afraid to go to Washington to better my future and create a way to serve others in the country that was giving me such amazing opportunities after such a horrific childhood.

Plus—and here's where the twentysomething in me showed—I had laid down some very hard-earned cash to buy a nice suit for the interview. A suit that, if I got the job, those people would be seeing a *lot* of. Maybe they would think it was a Steve Jobs vibe and that I just chose to wear the same thing every day to be efficient in my lifestyle. After all, no one ever *really* knew if Mr. Jobs just had one black turtleneck and one pair of Levi's or a hundred, right?

At the time, I was living in a trailer with way too many other guys who were also students. On campus, these homes-on-wheels were known as "the party trailers." Booze, pot, girls, and an endless game of *Madden NFL* on PlayStation. On the morning of September 12, I got up at five a.m., showered, put on my suit, and stepped around all the bodies sprawled across the floor. Whether that was where they had passed out or just where they decided to go to sleep, I tried hard not to disturb anyone as I left on my trip to downtown DC.

The interview went on as scheduled. It must have gone well because I got the job. They said yes to *me*.

Suddenly, I was a twenty-one-year-old economist working for a nationally respected organization in our nation's capital. *This meant I could finally stop waiting tables.*

I need to interject here that my dream job had always been to become a sports agent, representing pro athletes and negotiating multimillion-dollar deals for my heroes. That's why I was shocked when, about two months into my new job, a new opportunity came to the foundation, and they approached me with the proposition.

Play Ball? Pay Up!

There was this unique issue that had flown under the radar for years called "the jock tax." When professional athletes in any major sport traveled around the country to play, they were taxed for the work done in every state where they played, not, like the rest of us, solely based on the state where they lived as their primary residence. There was a question of fairness about this policy for players who had no choice about where they had to go to play their contracted sport.

Asked if I was willing to dive in and learn everything I could to make recommendations toward some sort of solution to this tax policy, I told them I'd have to think about it and get back to them. *Just kidding.* I wanted to see if you were paying attention. I said what? *Yes!*

I was ready to go full speed ahead, getting to dig into *two* of my passions: finances and sports. But I only knew one thing for sure about this specific subject of taxation: that I didn't know *anything* about it. But applying my modus operandi for life, I was not going to let that little bump in the road stop me. My advantage was that I walked in with zero preconceived ideas about any of this and could learn everything I needed to know. The very reason this issue had been brought to the Tax Foundation was because there was no expert on this topic. *Yet.*

One of the greatest principles I discovered while working on this project is that an expert is *not* a know-it-all. Experts just have to show what they know and what they *don't* know in a certain area of expertise. In fact, when you actually become an expert in any area, you aren't intimidated or afraid to say what you don't know. Because everyone sees how much you do know! Your work attests to the title you are given. You have nothing to prove because you already are who you say you are.

I became a regular at the Library of Congress, reading everything I could get my hands on that was related to this sports taxation issue. I called players. I called sports agents. I called accountants. Oddly, if any of them did take my call, after I explained what I was doing, they would typically laugh and say something like, "You're actually going to try to help these guys?" What was implied was this: "These millionaire players? See if you can help them save money by paying *less* in taxes?" And then insert sarcasm: "Oh, everyone will be sympathetic and get on board with you on *that*! This will be right up there with saving baby seals."

Yet, because I was the only guy to ever try to tackle this issue, as word spread, I was slowly becoming "the expert." With classic 1990s spiked blond hair and earrings, I had wrestled with the question of "Do I need to look like the stereotypical economist, or do I look like, well, *me*?" I decided to forego the standard fare expectations and say yes to being me.

In response to this jock tax issue being brought to light, my phone began to ring. Soon, I was quoted in the *Wall Street Journal*. I was interviewed on *SportsCenter*. *How about that? An economist on ESPN?* Eventually, the federal government got involved. From this platform, I started working with Senator Max Baucus from Montana, who chaired the Finance Committee, along with other congressional leaders. All this at twenty-one years old.

One particular highlight was when the Cincinnati City Council called me to testify. I recall using Shaquille O'Neal as my example, saying, "Shaq is paying a much higher percentage of taxes than his wealthy neighbors simply because he plays pro basketball for a living." While it was hard for those in authority to swallow helping these guys save money on their taxes, the real point was that the policy was simply not fair. It was arbitrary. The bottom line was that athletes were paying a lot more taxes than their neighbors, and tax policies should be fair for everyone. The playing field was *not* level. (Pun intended.)

The consequence of this unjust taxation was that athletes started realizing their reality and moving their primary residence to states where their taxation would be less. That's exactly what Shaq did. That was my point. Sometimes people laughed at me due to the subject matter and the argument, but often, these people would tell me I made a compelling argument with my presentation.

While many nonresident tax laws exist, states find it easier to figure out how much wealthy, high-profile professionals owe, but a snowball effect began in the sports world when this taxation policy began to go past the players who made millions. The practice of overtaxing spread when states started to track and charge others in these organizations: the coaching staff, then the junior coaching staff, and then the trainers. Then this same policy began to be true in music. It's just as easy to monitor Aerosmith's nationwide tour as it is the Milwaukee Bucks' road schedule, allowing states to tax traveling performers as they would athletes, especially considering singers like Steven Tyler are in the same tax bracket as LeBron James. I wanted people to consider what would happen if states began to enforce this same taxation policy for the ball boys and the roadies who are making twenty bucks an hour in all those states with their different tax rates.

During the time I was traveling and speaking about the jock tax, Major League Baseball was in the process of relocating the Montreal Expos. When Washington, DC, the proposed new location, announced its plan to implement "the country's most defined jock tax" to finance the stadium, Robert DuPuy, the MLB's president and chief operating officer at the time, called the idea "troublesome," and Bud Selig, the then–MLB Commissioner, announced he would consider San José, Costa Rica, for the team's relocation.[2] The tide began to turn, and my work started paying off. I was accomplishing exactly what the Tax Foundation does and had assigned me to do.

Because of this strange national recognition, doors started opening up for me with law firms and pro sports teams. Athletes began to reach out to me—some to thank me, others to offer me opportunities.

At the time, I was making decent money, so I purchased a townhome, my first real estate experience. The incredible thing about having my own place and living by myself was I could be in *any* room I wanted and leave *any* time I chose. I could run water any time for any reason. I could buy the food I wanted, eat what I wanted when I wanted. Because of the trauma of my childhood, what would be a very simple lifestyle to most was living like a king to me. The freedom, coupled with my perceived abundance, was life changing. I was grateful for my independence.

Regrets and Revelations

In late 2003, I was on the phone with my mom, telling her about all the crazy stuff that was happening to me. She was so proud. I could hear her smiling over the phone. I knew her face was beaming with pride in her son. When I finished with my update, Mom said, "David, I knew it. I knew all this would happen for you one day. I've hoped and prayed for this. All your dreams are coming true."

As we closed the conversation, Mom said, "David, I can't wait to see you again." I promised her that I would break away from the busyness and come "in the next few weeks, for sure."

At least, that was my plan.

But I never made the time to go, and on the evening of January 27, 2004, my stepmom called. She *never* called me, so I suspected something was up. She said, "David, I need to give you a couple of updates."

After some news about my dad and what he was doing, I was still suspicious of her call, so I asked, "Why are you *really* calling?"

Almost as if she were giving me an afterthought, she answered, "I also needed to tell you that your mom died today." *Yes, just like that.*

Now that I was in shock, my stepmom continued, "They need to find you because you're her life insurance beneficiary, and someone has to pay for the funeral." (Mom's policy was small, just enough to cover the expenses.)

Ironically, but not that surprisingly really, my mom had never taken off her engagement ring that my dad had given her. The funeral home had, of course, removed all of her jewelry. When I met with the director to handle the service details, he handed her ring to me. For me, it symbolized my mother's unconditional love that caused her to always look for the good in everyone and believe in the best in all circumstances. A very special family heirloom was born that day.

In May of 2004, four months after my mom passed, I, at twenty-four years old, was asked to speak at the sports and entertainment law conference in Baltimore, Maryland. Many of my sports heroes were going to be there. To say I was excited about this opportunity did not do my emotions justice.

The day before the event, I traveled to Baltimore, about two and a half hours north. I wanted to spend the night there so I could be rested and ready. Knowing I would have some rare free time at the hotel, I brought all my mail and bills to look over. While sifting through the various envelopes, I came across a reminder card for a multiple sclerosis fundraiser walk. The date was the next day, the same as my speaking event. As I read the details, something strange came over me. Conviction ran through me. Memories of my mother flooded my heart. Then an idea took hold and wouldn't let go.

I pulled out my laptop and emailed the person who had invited me to speak at the sports conference, writing, "I'm sorry, but I can't make it to the event to speak. I need to take part in an MS walk to honor my mom." I said a bit more, but that was the gist.

Later, the person called. I didn't answer but let it go to voicemail. A message I knew I did not want to listen to, at least not yet.

The next day, to say no to my ego, my driving ambition, and my rise to success, I said yes to my mom. I said yes to a self-sacrificing day so I could honor *her* life. In a strange way, while at the walk, I felt like I had spent the entire day with my mother. I talked aloud to her. I grieved her death. I celebrated her life. Aloud, I said all the things I had been needing to say, everything I had been needing to *hear* myself say.

I finally confessed to her what had been in my heart for months: my one regret in life (and still is to this day) is that I did not make the time to go visit my mom after she said how much she wanted to see me. I had promised her that I would come soon. But I didn't. I won't know until I get to heaven if my mom knew how sick she actually was. But even if she did, she wouldn't have said because she wouldn't have wanted me to worry about her.

Following that phone call between Mom and me, due to my daily decision to say no to her over those next few weeks, I was not able to say goodbye to the *one* person who I absolutely knew had loved me my entire life. The *one* person who was always proud of me, no matter what. The *one* person I saw express real faith in a God of love.

Yes, I had gone to the funeral. I had stood alone at the open casket. Time seemed to stop as I viewed her too-young-to-die, fifty-two-year-old body with her long, flowing brown hair. And I cried. In fact, I cried for days after that. But the tears were just as much out of regret as grief. Maybe more.

When someone dies, you don't get a second chance. You don't get a do-over. It's death, the sole force that separates us from this life. Saying goodbye while looking into someone's eyes is still tough, but it can help remove the regrets. In some odd way, my intentional choice to set aside my ascent to success to do the MS walk made me feel like I had finally chosen my mom over me. I overcame my no of the past with a yes today. That decision was also the first time I felt like I had made the choice to love someone unconditionally.

Upon hearing what I had done that day, some of my friends protested, "What! You picked a charity walk over giving the talk of a lifetime? You just blew your biggest opportunity!"

When they asked if the person who invited me to speak understood, I answered honestly, "No. He's not too happy with me. He said he never should have given such a big opportunity and responsibility to such a young kid. He thought I was irresponsible and ungrateful for his offer."

Regardless of anyone's opinion about whether I did the right thing that day or not, this wasn't about a right-or-wrong situation but a what-I-have-to-do decision to be right with *me*. The memories of my mother coupled with the goodbye I so desperately needed to express.

Understanding my choice that day caused me to rethink my priorities. One of my friends made a suggestion. "David, you love people. You obviously value relationships. Plus, now that you've bought your own place, you seem to really enjoy real estate. Like, you know a lot about it." (That was true but only for the reason that I was the first one in our friend group to buy a house and had done my due diligence to find the right buy. After all, I was an economist.)

Another friend chimed in, "Yeah, that's right, David. You should look into real estate."

In what seemed to be a random suggestion, my friends had caused me to think seriously about a different career path. As an economist, I was making about $45,000 a year. Considering the DC cost of living, after my mortgage was paid, my utilities and food, my Metro card, and trying to stay in a decent suit to play the part, I was either breaking even or upside-down every month. Taking their advice, I began to look into getting my real estate license. After the fast-paced life in the Northeast for close to twenty-five years, dreams of a slower pace somewhere with a lower cost of living actually began to appeal to me. A total life makeover felt right.

During those days of reevaluation and transition, the girl I was dating exclusively at the time told me that she was going to leave Virginia and move to Charlotte, North Carolina.

Unsure of what to do next and sincerely second-guessing what life might look like if I got my law degree, I made another seemingly rash decision. I put my town-home up for sale and quicky sold it for a handsome profit. Using money made from, interestingly enough, my first successful real estate deal, I said goodbye to the high life in DC, set fire to my big plans, and decided to follow a girl to a city I knew nothing about.

I said yes to starting a new chapter in my life. But little did I know that God was about to start writing an entirely different story.

3

OLD WOUNDS AND NEW STARTS

With what little I owned packed into my car, I began the drive out of DC. For miles, my eyes cut back and forth between the windshield and the rearview mirror. My life in the capital city was slowly fading away. A fascinating thing about our world is the changing perspective. When we are leaving something behind, the image grows smaller while what we're headed toward slowly grows larger and more visible. I think there was a part of me that was hoping this crazy decision would leave the pain and trauma of my upbringing in the past and allow me to embrace a new life of freedom and, dare I say it, blessing.

On the four-hundred-mile drive to Charlotte, my thoughts jumped between random and strategic. I was no longer on speaking terms with the God of my father—the one in the Torah—or my mother—the one from the New Testament, hanging on the cross. Even though I had delayed seeing my mom, knowing that God allowed her to die without me being able to say goodbye was the absolute last straw. Just more evidence that whoever he is was out to get me. But as angry as I was, I also could *not* seem to dismiss my thoughts and questions about him either.

Pushing aside my fight with religion for the moment, next up on my drive south, I made a decision to form my first set of foundational standards. In my new life in Charlotte, I vowed that I would do the following.

1. Be a Friend

Going someplace where I knew no one, outside of the girl I was chasing, I decided my number one goal when I arrived was to make *one* friend as soon as possible. One person—I would start there. I had never had many friends growing up. I had college buddies. I had a small group of personal friends in DC with lots of "business friends," many of whom I always questioned whether I could really trust. In starting over, I wanted to have as many *authentic* relationships as I could.

I knew I needed contacts, a network, all those necessary elements to have a successful career. But my real goal was to make friends by *being* a friend. That's how I wanted to build my personal and professional foundation in Charlotte.

2. Be an Expert

If I was going to get established in real estate there, I was determined to excel in the market. Applying everything I had learned from becoming the "jock tax expert" to my new career, I would become a voracious student of the industry while freely admitting what I did not know—yet. Over time, I wanted to create a knowledge base from my growing network of new friends, building off standard number one and adding value to all my friendships.

3. Be Present

Growing up feeling invisible for so many years and lacking the physical and emotional presence of my parents, I was determined to be present in every way, wherever I was. A strange dynamic about us as people is how we can be sitting in a boardroom around a table with ten people mapping out a business plan, but our thoughts can be at home on the couch or on a beach with a friend or even imagining ourselves in a different career. Our brains can take us where our hearts want to be at any given point in time. That's exactly why we can be with someone and the person can suddenly ask, "Hey…where are you?" People can obviously see a physical presence yet sense there is no presence of mind. My goal was that my friends and clients would always see that I was right there with them in the moment. Focused. Intentional.

Prior to moving, I had decided to take some of the money I made from the sale of my townhome in DC and make a down payment on a townhome in Charlotte. I had googled real estate agencies, and the number one hit in my search was Allen Tate Realtors. I connected with an agent there and found my new home, agreeing to buy sight unseen from the online pictures. But in the same transaction, I also created a connection with the largest agency in my new hometown.

One Hundred Houses and a Broken Heart

On May 3, 2005, just two days after I moved to Charlotte, I began real estate school. During that first week, I arranged a meeting with the head sales manager at Allen Tate Realtors. If they had the number one position in the search engine, then that's where I wanted to be. I told her my plan of going into real estate and inquired about getting on with their company. We made an appointment, and I sat down to meet with her. I'll never forget that brief Q and A.

"David, do you know how much a first-year agent here makes on average?"

I said no.

She stated, "$15,000." Continuing, she said, "Second year?" She paused, "$18,000." Pausing again for dramatic effect, she then asked, "Want to know what happens in year three?"

I swallowed hard and meekly answered, "Uh, yes."

Delivering what she assumed would be her knock-out punch, in a bit of an ominous tone, the sales manager stated, "Most people don't make it to year three."

Boom! Drop the mic, ma'am. That…was…amazing!

Here's what she had no way of knowing about me: my background of having nothing, coupled with my belief in sacrificing to get where I knew I needed to go, led me to think, *Wow, $15,000, huh? I can make that work. Then in year two, I can make even more? Sign me up!* What she seemed to hope would be a sobering wake-up call, scare tactic, and young-dreamer reality check was just a normal day in the life of David Hoffman. I wasn't after money; I wanted a new life.

I smiled and politely offered, "Okay, well, you know, I am *not* most people. I think I understand what it will take. Let me ask—provided someone survives the first two lean years—what can an agent make in the third year?"

She answered, "$60,000."

I smiled and said, "Okay, I can live a really great life on $60,000. But I think I'm going to do better than that."

Please understand, while I know full well such a response can be read and interpreted as cockiness or arrogance, I just had a do-or-die confidence that I had crafted in the hardball world of DC. I believed that if I was given a shot, I could work hard enough and learn enough to produce, both for the company and for myself.

To what extent she thought she was taking a chance, I don't know, but she said yes.

When I graduated and got my real estate license, I was proud to be awarded "Most Likely to Succeed." Assuming I needed to look like a young, successful real estate agent in the Bible Belt rather than a hip, young DC tax expert who could look cool on ESPN, I ditched the earrings, deconstructed my spiked-up hair, and gave in to the classic comb-over to the side, successfully adding about five years to my baby face. *Okay, three.* I already had the nice suits purchased from clearance racks, so that was a big win on the fashion side.

I started as an agent for Tate in the summer of 2005. In my first full year, I closed forty-six deals. You ask, *How much did an agent who closed forty-six deals make in 2005 in Charlotte, North Carolina?* Well, if you're thinking more than $15,000, you'd be right. I made $200,000 that first year. My second year, I made $250,000. From 2005 to 2008, I was one of the top-producing agents and the youngest. While I'm not accustomed to, nor comfortable with, throwing out my sales numbers, I'm only giving you these for my first two years to offer some sort of perspective of what I was told versus where I ended up. To me, it simply establishes credibility for the principles I will share. I believe they can work for anyone. They are not at all exclusive to me.

Halfway through my second year, I received a letter in the mail from the owner, Allen Tate himself. At the time, I was just one young agent within the company's huge roster. Inside was a handwritten note that simply said, "Congratulations on a great eighteen months. I'd love to meet you sometime."

Just like the conversation with my professor back at George Mason, my immediate response was "Yes!" quickly followed up with "Wow, why *me*?" Right away, I reached out to Mr. Tate's office and scheduled a meeting. From that first visit together, we talked easily and became close. What I appreciated most about Allen was his leadership style—in the marketplace and the community. He was able to walk that fine line of clearly commanding the helm in so many different places while also never stepping on anyone's toes. Now that he's passed, I will always be grateful to him for reaching out to me, for his mentorship over the years, and for being the father figure I never had.

Now, some of you are thinking, *This is great, David, but what about the girl, the one you followed to Charlotte?* Okay, so if I was one of the top-producing salespeople during my first three years in real estate, what do you think might have suffered in what was supposed to be my priority relationship? Yep, as I dove headfirst into my new adventure as a real estate entrepreneur, one day she told me we needed to talk. When a woman tells a man, "We need to talk," that is rarely a good-news moment. We definitely had experienced some bumps in the road, but as an incurable glass-half-full, positive thinker, I wasn't sure what she was going to say to me.

After we sat down, she stated, "David, you're a good person." *Why is it that statement never feels good?* "In fact, you're my best friend. You are definitely present in your business. I see that. But you are *not* present with me…and I need someone to *be* present with me, to *want* to be present with me…*without* me having to ask." Bottom line—that night was the beginning of the end. I'm grateful to say neither of us burned the bridge, but our time together was over.

That moment was a wake-up call for me because the person I was supposed to make feel the most secure by my presence said I wasn't available. I had violated my own standard number three, meaning I had also unknowingly violated standard number one. I had put my career, my ambition, over a relationship, over my best friend. I determined that night to learn from that mistake and be mindful to never let it happen again, if and when I had another shot at a woman choosing to love me.

David, I'd Like You to Meet Jesus

In a later chapter, I'll be telling you much more about the economic crash of 2008 and 2009, but for now, I want to continue sharing about my personal life. In fact, the most important event in my life. One that overshadows any other relationship or any successful venture.

During that massive downturn in the real estate business, one of my new friends, Justin Reeder, founder of a successful company and a nonprofit ministry called Love Life, called to check on me. Like so many of my relationships, Justin started out as a client. After a few minutes of catch-up, he asked, "Hey, David, why don't you come to church with me?" I knew his dad was a pastor in Orlando, that he was a Christian, and that he went to church regularly. Being in the Bible Belt, I had already realized Charlotte was far more of a faith community than the places I had lived before. So getting invited to church by a friend was not an *if* but a *when*. Today was evidently *my* when.

I decided to set my beef with God aside, honor my friend Justin, and say yes.

During the pastor's message, he asked some questions, "Have you fallen lately? Are you going through a crisis in a relationship? Are you struggling with life?" What he intended as rhetorical I took as personal. My mind began to race and ask, *Did Justin tell the pastor about me? Is this a setup? This is a really big church, but how could there possibly be anyone else here that has these exact same issues? Why is he talking about me, to me, in front of everyone?* I kept my paranoid thoughts and questions to myself, but something began to stir in my heart.

A couple of days later, Justin asked me to meet him for lunch. As the server took our plates away, my friend smiled, looked me right in the eyes, and said, "David, it's your time."

Confused, I responded, "My time? What do you mean?"

With an obvious deep sincerity and compassion, he answered, "David, I've known you for a while now. I know your story, and God knows your story. You've tried to live your own way for so long. You just need to give your life to Jesus. He's at work here and has always been there for you. I can't let my brother go another day without knowing the Lord. So today's *your* day. You need to know him. This is your day to give your life to Jesus, just like I have, just like the pastor talked about Sunday."

I was intrigued as we kept talking. I asked a few questions, and he offered great answers. Bottom line—everything began to make sense, to fall into place. Even my memorization of the Torah now seemed to have a context. The questions that had been stirring in my heart finally found someone who had a real answer. In a moment at a restaurant table, suddenly, as I began to quietly cry, I realized that God was not my dad's or my mom's or some distant entity or at a Mets game. He was right there, somehow present in Justin's words and care, ready to receive *me.*

Once and for all, I dropped my guard and surrendered to the God I had hated for so many years. I finally realized, of all the many lies I had been told, the biggest was the one I had told myself—that he couldn't possibly love *me.* My mom's prayers, which I undoubtedly know she offered up countless times from her wheelchair in that small apartment, were answered in that moment.

Praying with Justin, I invited Jesus Christ to take over this mess of a life I had lived. I opened my heart and received the greatest love available to anyone. The truth of the New Testament connected to the Torah I had memorized as a child to bring Scripture to life in me. I accepted the Father I had never known or understood. Finally as an adult, I felt the peace of being accepted and wanted as a chosen child of the King with an eternal inheritance and a home in heaven. All made possible by the Jesus who not only hung on the cross and died for my sins, like the little statue in my mom's home, but who also defeated sin and death and rose from the grave. All so I might have life.

> There is no condemnation for those who belong to Christ Jesus. And because you belong to him, the power of the life-giving Spirit has freed you from the power of sin that leads to death. The law of Moses was unable to save us because of the weakness of our sinful nature. So God did what the law could not do. He sent his own Son in a body like the bodies we sinners have. And in that body God declared an end to sin's control over us by giving his Son as a sacrifice for our sins. (Romans 8:1–3)

David, I'd Like You to Meet Jessica

One of the you-can't-write-stuff-this-good friendships I had made in Charlotte was a nationally known pro wrestler, a larger-than-life character. *Yes, really.* (I've chosen to keep his name confidential.) The next night after I gave my life to Christ, he invited me to dinner to help him celebrate his sixtieth birthday. He picked me up in a limo, and we went to a high-end steak house.

The wrestler invited his driver, whom he knew well, to join us. After we had walked in and he surveyed the room, the driver pointed to a woman seated at the bar with a friend and said, "See her? She's mine tonight." Evidently, walking over to ladies and name-dropping that you work for a professional wrestler had somehow become his successful pick-up line.

After we finished our meal, he went to the bar and began talking to her. When he had to go to the restroom, he motioned for me to "hold his seat for him." Complying, I got up, walked over, and sat down next to this beautiful girl. Not accustomed to the rules of the game, I said, "Hey, I'm sorry about him. He's not actually my friend. I'm with that guy over there, his boss. I apologize if he's bothering you. By the way, I'm David."

She smiled and said, "Hi, I'm Jessica."

We began the small talk with the typical what-do-you-do questions. After a few minutes, her friend—who probably was quickly getting bored and wanting to exit before the limo driver returned—said to her, "Let's get out of here."

As they were gathering their things to leave, I said, "Well, I just wanted to apologize for the intrusion. This may sound bad, too, but here's my card." Even though I sold real estate, I didn't make a practice of handing out business cards. But for some reason, I gave one to her. She smiled, took the card, and said goodbye.

After a great evening of celebration, my friend and his driver took me back to my house. At 2:30 in the morning, I got a text from the beautiful girl at the bar that read, "First, this isn't what you think, but it was a pleasure talking with you tonight. Since we only had a few minutes together, I'd like to do it again sometime." Let's just say I was good with that.

We set up a date. Then another. And another. One evening while talking, Jessica mentioned that she went to church. Of course, I was now good with that too. I asked her where, and she answered with the name of the same church I had visited and where I first heard the gospel. She was there that morning, sitting somewhere near me. I shared with Jessica about my new decision to follow Christ, and we talked about our faith. Another strong connection.

In getting to know one another, I learned that she had her own story of family trauma. Because of how we both grew up, we were equally prepared for the changes in our income and lifestyle while the economy was so bad in 2009. I found it such a blessing that she just wanted quality time with me. We didn't *need* anything. We just enjoyed being together.

Jessica saw something in me that was more than just sales numbers or money or the other material things for which a lot of people sought me out. She looked past all that and saw me simply for who I was. For the first time in my life, I felt like someone saw my heart the way my mom had.

While there was obvious romance and chemistry, we also became best friends. We went to church together every Sunday. (By that time, the pastor had quit talking about me.) We regularly served in the community together, volunteering for various charities, service projects, and ministries.

But my toxic history with distrust and sensitivity to my past, coupled with a fierce sense of independence as I had hit thirty years old, began to create distance between us, just as it had with the girl I had followed to Charlotte. We slowly began to lose touch, talking and seeing each other less and less often. That was all on me. I was scared of getting too close to someone. My fear of abandonment and rejection created a roadblock in moving forward with the woman I had started to realize I was falling in love with. Losing my mom was devastating. I couldn't handle losing Jessica too. So I decided that maybe it was best to not even let myself be placed in that position. Counselors call that *self-sabotage*.

But seemingly out of the blue one day, Jessica called me. "Hey, I want to buy a house. Would you help me?" Of course, I agreed, which allowed for a natural reconnection. We began to spend time together again. While we still focused on serving others, we made a lot more intentional time for us. That led to us *both* knowing we had fallen in love. In fact, she told me first, which gave me the reassurance I needed to profess my love for her too. For the first time in my life, I was trusting someone past my ability to risk emotionally.

On Christmas Day 2011, we were at her grandparents' farm. When we got to her grandfather's tractor, I asked, "Hey, why don't you jump up there, and I'll take your picture?"

When she got into place, I got down on one knee and reached in my pocket for her to think I was grabbing my phone. But instead, I took out a ring box and proposed right there. *And you probably thought tractors couldn't be romantic.*

In February of 2009, within a twenty-four-hour time frame, I met my Abba Father.

I met my Savior and Lord, Jesus.

I met the love of my life, Jessica.

Within the span of a day, God poured out his love on my life, changing—literally—everything.

No, I wasn't miraculously healed of all the hurts of my past, but I was introduced to heavenly and human manifestations of his love to begin the journey of my new life. For the first time, I believed God's promise in Jeremiah 29:11 was meant for me: "'For I know the plans I have for you,' declares the Lord, 'plans to prosper you and not to harm you, plans to give you hope and a future'" (NIV).

4

JESSICA'S STORY

The evening David and I met, our exchange was quick and surface. But he *had* given me his business card. So I'm going to be honest—I reached out to him later that night because I thought he was handsome. Plus, especially in how he apologized for the aggressive limo driver, I could see he was clearly a true gentleman.

Agreeing to go out, we set up a brunch date for the weekend. We lived in the same area of Charlotte and then, of course, found out in conversation that he had been going to the church where I went.

One of the reasons David and I connected so quickly was because we shared similar backgrounds. On that first date, he really opened up to me about the abuse and neglect he had suffered growing up. I was impressed that he was so vulnerable, much more than most men would think about being. He was humble, and his approach was refreshing to me.

As I listened intently to his story, I remember thinking to myself, *Wow, it's like we had the same kind of childhood.*

From birth, I was in a dangerous situation in my parents' home primarily because of my stepfather. After an incident of sexual abuse when I was just four years old, my mother took me to the hospital. Seeing the nature of my injuries and my overall frailty, the hospital staff called child protection services to intervene. Due to the threat to my safety if I returned to my home, the court granted guardianship of me to my grandparents on my mom's side. I never went back to my parents. Thank God that my grandparents were able to take custody of me and I wasn't placed into the foster care system. Plus, knowing she needed to protect her daughter, my mom fully supported my going to live with her parents.

So I grew up on their family farm, and fortunately, I have no memories of my childhood prior to going to their home. To me, my grandparents *were* my parents. They both, most especially my grandmother, showed me Jesus. My mother always lived close to us and would visit. To this day, we have a good relationship and are very close. I want her to be in the lives of our sons and for them to know her.

My grandfather had quit school when he was in the sixth grade to work on the farm. Because of that choice, he had never learned how to read. He worked the land his entire life and was just the sweetest, friendliest, greatest man to me.

My grandmother took me to church services at least twice a week. I have vivid memories of her standing during worship, eyes closed, singing with both hands lifted high. She loved Jesus, and I saw that love lived out firsthand every day as she took care of me.

That is, until I was twelve years old and our lives took a horrible turn. My grandmother was in a bad car wreck, hit by a drunk driver. She was airlifted to the hospital and placed on life support while in a coma. No one thought she would pull through. After being in the hospital for two months, she survived but had suffered severe brain damage.

While she was still able to walk, she was not very mobile. Refusing to use a walker, she would often lose her balance and fall. She could still talk, but her communication skills were greatly challenged. She also lost most of her memory. She had no recollection of raising me. The *only* thing she seemed to remember well was that she loved Jesus. So while her body and mind were forever devastated by the tragedy, her spirit was still healthy and fully intact. A reminder that God created us with three distinct aspects as a reflection of the Trinity, and in our fallen state, only our spirits are the eternal part.

The foundation of my life had suddenly been ripped right out from under me. But this time, I was *very* aware of what was happening to my family. My grandfather was placed in the terrible position of having to take care of the farm and now also his paralyzed wife. His overwhelming burden left me essentially having to raise myself. While, of course, still very loved and not at all abandoned, I just felt like life was out to get me. *Twice,* I had to suffer the fate of having my family taken from me. I had been removed from my parents, and now, I felt like my grandparents had been removed too.

As I entered my teenage years, I began to get angry at God. Having to watch someone who loved me and whom I loved so much, someone who was so close to Jesus, suffer at the hands of evil was more than I could handle. Sound familiar? I felt like that drunk driver had destroyed my life, too, but no one could *see* my debilitating injuries. The seeds of rebellion were becoming deeply rooted in my heart, pushing me away from *any* faith. My life had become much like David's life, knowing his mother's deep love for Christ, all while enduring the life both of them were forced to live for years. That was just like me and my grandmother. That's why I quickly understood him. In the heart of a child, trying to resolve that conflict, to reconcile that struggle, feels almost impossible. Insurmountable.

Behold, I Stand at the Door and Knock

Throughout high school, my rebellion and anger grew worse. Following graduation, wanting desperately to be the first person in our family to go to college, I started working and putting myself through school. But after leaving home and becoming independent, I started down a bad path. Like so many kids who go away to school, partying became my major *and* my minor.

One day, after I had been up all night drinking with friends, we were carrying the party into the next morning when there was a knock on our door. The person asked for *me* by name. I had no idea who she was. The lady looked at me with grace and compassion, no judgment in her eyes, and said, "I was told to come here and pray with you. I'm not here for any other reason. Not asking anything. I'm just supposed to pray for you."

Surprised, and probably tapping into something deep in my spirit that connected back to my grandmother's influence and prayers, I agreed and invited her in. The woman did exactly as she promised. No tricks. No manipulation. True to her word, she just prayed for me. And, miraculously, God's Spirit moved in my heart. She *had* clearly been sent. Nothing else made sense.

We read about those divine crossroads moments throughout Scripture. At the burning bush. In the winepress. Out in the field. On the seashore. The Damascus road. The places where God suddenly shows up unannounced and disrupts life forever. That morning was mine, when a stranger came to my door after another hopeless night of drunken partying. In that woman's presence, I felt like God had come after me. Like the shepherd leaving the ninety-nine to go after the one lost sheep. Like the prodigal being given his aha moment in the pigsty to go back home. I knew I had to reconcile with the one parent who had never abused me and had never been taken from me. The One from whom no tragedy or trauma could ever separate me—my Father in heaven.

I knew I had to let go of the past, the anger, the rebellion, and get my heart right with God. I had to restore my life with the same Jesus my grandmother loved so deeply. I needed to learn to trust him the way she did. Because now, I could see how much he obviously loved *me*.

So, with my hand in his, we made the long walk back home to my faith. Out of obedience, I stopped the partying. I started going to church. I began the one-eighty turn to the life he created me to experience.

Allow me to insert a flashback moment here. When I was a little girl, someone at my grandmother's church had prophesied that one day I would rebel from God but then come back to Christ and be restored to him. I actually have the recording of that prophecy from the church. I kept it. Going back to listen to that tape, to hear those words, the voice speaking into my future as a child, is both surreal and divine. A prophecy that most certainly came to pass.

You Just Know

When I graduated college, I went into the staffing business, meaning I helped employers find qualified candidates in a wide variety of industries. My very first job was in construction. I would drive up to building sites in a pickup and be *very* out of place among the work crews. I often got the stop-and-stare, what-are-*you*-doing-here looks.

As I continued to grow my business, I began to work with Goodwill Industries, launching a personalized staffing program. I opened three offices for them in different locations and managed those sites. I also kept working with various corporations to find talent and initiate training programs. That was my career when I met David.

Now that you know how my story connects to his, let's go back to our first date.

I was still somewhat new in my spiritual journey, so when he opened up to me and I realized David was in a very similar place in life from a very similar past, I felt a unique connection. Hearing about his success in business after coming out of poverty resonated with me, too, as I was working hard to excel in my own opportunities. Like David, I was grateful for the chance to change the legacy of my family.

I was amazed to hear how he had just recently come to Christ from a Jewish background and was hungry to grow and learn like me. After David had finished telling his story, I shared enough for him to see how much we had in common, although I saved all of my story for another time.

In the spirit of full disclosure here, on that first date, somehow I knew David was "the one." You know, when you're single and couples tell you, "Oh, you'll just know," that can be really frustrating because you wonder, *How will I "just know"?* Yet when you do meet "the one" and you "just know," you get it. And how *could* you possibly know before that moment? Like they say, I *just knew.*

But at the time, we were not in the same place emotionally. His timing and mine weren't yet aligned. I was ready to settle down, but I could see David wasn't there. So I needed to be patient and just wait. God would show us together what to do and when.

We were never officially boyfriend and girlfriend that first year. Though exclusive, we kept things casual. There were even a couple of months when we took a break and didn't see each other. But in the absence, my heart was still with him. We also hadn't said that we loved each other even though I knew that's what I was feeling.

Somewhere into our third month apart, knowing what a great real estate agent David was, I reached out and told him I was ready to buy a house. Now, I didn't really *want* to buy a house. But I knew it would be a good investment. And I *could*. So I *did*. As David was helping me look, we started talking again. Then we started dating again. And then we became "relationship official." Oh, and yeah, I also bought a house.

David was involved with the Leukemia & Lymphoma Society in Charlotte. During our dating season, he was nominated for their Man of the Year award. I attended all those events with him. We also got involved together with the Junior Chamber of Commerce in Charlotte, a young professionals' organization, and did volunteer work with Goodwill. Of course, wanting to grow in our faith, we went to church together. One of the ongoing aspects of our lives that started back then has been serving together.

Dropping "I Love You"

On Thanksgiving 2009, I had spent the day with my family. That evening I planned a Friendsgiving, as it's come to be called, with David because I knew we were not yet at the place of inviting him home for the holidays, but I also knew he had no family to go to.

In the late afternoon, I drove home to my new house and cooked another Thanksgiving meal for David and a few of our friends. That evening, after everyone had left, with a grin, he said, "You know, you can tell me you love me. It's okay if you want to." He kept playfully pressing me. Finally, I responded, "All right…I do. I love you."

David smiled. And then…(are you ready, ladies?)…he said…*nothing*. He didn't reciprocate, creating an awkward silence. I didn't regret telling him because it had been true for me for a long time. But a girl expects an "I love you" back. No, you want more than an "I love you" if you say it first. You want an I'm-crazy-about-you-I-can't-live-without-you-and-you-are-the-only-one-for-me-Matthew-McConaughey-rom-com-all-right-all-right-all-right kind of "I love you!" Am I right?

But I guess he just had to sleep on it because when we got together the next day, David told me he loved me too. In all seriousness, I knew more than anyone the deep insecurities and distrust that he had to overcome to trust me, as well as himself, enough to say words that were incredibly important to him: I love you. That level of commitment meant a great deal to us both and was an expression of each of our personal growth and healing.

By the next year, when the holidays rolled around, we had both the commitment and comfort level for David to be with my family. On Christmas Day 2011 at my grandparents' farm, he proposed, and I said yes. When he suggested he take my picture on the tractor, I noticed he suddenly got nervous, so I knew something was up. But I was not expecting him to pop the question that day.

Here's where I turned the tables on him from the delayed "I love you" moment. After we got engaged at Christmas, I wanted a spring wedding. Three or four months was not enough time to put everything together. So I made *him* wait. Until the *following* spring. Girls win.

We were married in March of 2013. Like David always says, relationships over rules. Another story of two people only God could put together. Another story only he could write.

5

BOLD CHOICES, BROKEN CHAINS

Now that you've read my wife's story, I want to pick mine back up in the most challenging season I've ever experienced in the real estate market.

Life seems to follow a series of bell curves. What goes up must come down. I promised in a previous chapter that I would talk about the economic crash in greater detail. Well, if you lived on Planet Earth in 2008, you already have some idea of what happened to me then. Following the marketplace, real estate took a nosedive. The bubble burst, and the shrapnel took a bunch of people out in a very short amount of time.

Like so many agents, I had to find some kind of new normal. By 2009, even with the market at an all-time low, I actually managed to sell thirty-one properties, closing two to three a month. For a lot of agents, depending on the area where they sell, that number would still be a great year, any year. But it was a major setback for the volume I had become accustomed to producing. I was still able to earn over the six-figure mark in a year when so many agents got completely out of the business. I have always pushed myself to prove that if you give your all, regardless of external factors, you can sustain and find a way to thrive.

But even with strong sales for that time, the crash created a serious financial challenge for me. I had made the very common human error when one goes from having little to quickly being handed a lot. Regardless of the profession or your circumstances, the response can be the same. Whether $30,000 to $100,000 or $100,000 to $2 million, whether winning the lottery, receiving an inheritance, getting the big contract, settling a lawsuit, or just market timing, most of us don't handle sudden windfalls very well.

In my first year of sales, when the money started pouring in, I sold the townhome and bought a big house. I got the impressive car to drive clients around in. I went out to eat at nice restaurants almost every night. Hanging with high-profile people, riding in Lincoln Town Cars, going to parties, concerts, and clubs—experiencing the side of life I never dreamed I would be able to live. In a weird way, I felt like this was some sort of revenge for how I was treated growing up, that I somehow "deserved" this new life. But entitlement is one of the most dangerous things that can happen to the human soul.

Even still, getting hit hard was my norm, and I could at least fall back on my old paradigm of adjusting to living on a lot less. While I did my best to sell all the properties I could, I began to pour even more of my time and energy into my three standards: Be a friend. Be the expert. Be present.

I offered a listening ear to people who were hurting.
I extended a helping hand to people in need.

I encouraged and coached those in the industry who were questioning their career choice.

I gave time to charities and foundations.

I hosted fundraisers even though I wasn't making as much money at the time.

I made more friends, grew deeper relationships with the ones I already had, and broadened my network through service.

At one point, four or five friends who were struggling financially were living with me for free in my big house. I had been given resources, and I was now trying to share them.

As the tables turned so badly for so many in the 2008–2009 crash, here was my wake-up call story. I was at dinner with several people at a nice restaurant. To no surprise, my credit card had the New York Yankees logo emblazoned on it. When the bill came, I handed the server that card. A few minutes later, he came back to the table with it in his hand, smiling and sort of jokingly whispered to me, "Sorry, I'm a Red Sox fan. Your card was declined."

Knowing everyone at the table likely heard him, I laughed and said, "What? There's no way. There must be a problem."

The server asked, "Do you have another card I can try?"

I answered, "No, try that one again in a few minutes. I'm sure it will go through." He walked away, and the conversation continued.

But he quickly returned, shook his head, and handed the card back to me. I excused myself and stepped into a quiet corner to call the customer service number of the bank where my accounts were linked to my card. The rep pulled up my information and then asked, "Mr. Hoffman, we recently sent you a letter. Have you not gotten it?"

"No, not yet," I answered, puzzled. "What does the letter say?"

He then asked, "Are you still a real estate broker?"

Okay, this was getting weird. "Yes, I am."

The rep continued the questions, "Well, do you have another job?"

Now, I was getting perturbed by the personal inquiry. "No. I don't have another job. That's my career."

To that answer, he started reading the script off my account details, "The bank made the decision that your profession is no longer secure enough for your credit limit, which has been significantly reduced. That's why your card was declined."

Trying not to cry on the phone, I started pleading with the guy to add another hundred bucks to my limit just to pay for dinner. But the answer was firm: "I'm really sorry, sir. I have clear instructions here. That is not possible."

Humiliated, I had to call a friend to bring me money for dinner. By the way, that's a real friend. From a quarter of a million in sales commissions to "Hey, man, can you bring me a hundred bucks because my card was declined, and I can't leave the restaurant?" Nothing quite like a good humbling with dinner. I realized it was high time for me to find the balance, and, looking back, that is yet another moment I am grateful that the Lord allowed to discipline me.

Growing Pains

As the economy and the market began to recover heading into 2011, my business came roaring back quickly because all my relationships were not only still in place but also stronger than ever. Of course, not all of them were true friendships, but I did have a lot of authentic connections. People said things like, "You were there for me when the market was down. You were honest with me about your own challenges, so I want to work with you." Or "I want to refer you to someone." While I never made a conscious decision to serve people for my own benefit down the road, that's just a basic reap-what-you-sow principle of life. As the old saying goes, "People don't care how much you know (the expert) until they know how much you care (the friend)." Crawling out of the crash, I saw that truth played out firsthand.

By 2012, as the economy and the market were once again healthy and my sales were back to record numbers, a close friend told me, "David, you have too much business for one agent to handle and so many relationships to try to serve everyone well. I know you're planning to marry Jessica and have a family, sooner than later. I know your story, so I also know how much you want to be the present husband that your mom never had with your father. You want to be a great dad to your kids one day. With the Keller Williams model, you can build a team and not have to be 'all things to all people.' You can hire good folks to work in their gifts around you as you lead your own team while staying present right where you are."

Later in the year, he invited me to a gathering at a home to introduce me to some local leaders with Keller Williams, the national franchise realty group. Following that evening, and after a lot of prayer and discussion with Jessica, I realized it was time for me to move out on my own and build my own business. One of the great guidelines of entrepreneurship is to expand when you have maxed out your current opportunities. My friend was right. It *was* my time, and God confirmed the new call.

Without a noncompete clause in place at Tate, I had always been free to move, but I valued the relationship so much that my loyalty had driven me to stay. But on Friday, March 1, 2013, I told Mr. Tate I was leaving his fold to go out on my own. I had an email ready to go out to all my clients as soon as I had spoken with him.

That weekend, I intentionally didn't look at my phone until Monday morning because I was concerned about people's responses. I had left the number one firm in the metro-Charlotte area that was owned by my business mentor. After eight years with the company, I was well aware that no matter how successful anyone may have been, relationships can disappear quickly when you make a move. But when I finally got up the courage to turn my phone back on, I was pleasantly surprised that the feedback was very positive. There was nothing but encouragement and affirmation for my leap of faith. The move appeared to make sense to everyone and felt right.

So, if you haven't already connected the dots, yes, I launched my own real estate business in the same month that Jessica and I got married. I firmly believed that God wanted this new facet of my life in place before we began our new life together.

When we listen to the Holy Spirit, he will help us get our life not only right but also in the right *order*. Having my own realty team would help me accomplish my personal as well as my business goals. From day one, I have had the blessing and privilege to surround myself with amazing and talented people.

I think it took Mr. Tate a while to accept my decision. About six months after I was gone, he reached out and told me that he was proud of me. While the move was difficult for both of us and a bit challenging at first for our relationship, we both knew it was my time to grow. I received his words with gratitude and humility, as I had any time he gifted me with an affirmation.

The Whys and the What-Ifs

It turned out that launching my new business and getting married weren't the only reasons God had called me to step out. He alone knew what else was coming our way. Just a few weeks after our wedding, Jessica wasn't feeling well and immediately became suspicious that something unusual was going on with her body. A pregnancy test and a little math determined we had conceived *on* our honeymoon.

So, adding to all the newness in our lives, suddenly we were also navigating a pregnancy. We were quickly swimming in the deep end. Jessica had a difficult nine months from being sick a lot and struggling health-wise throughout. But on January 6, 2014, our son, Kane, was born.

In 2015, we got pregnant with our second child. At five months, we knew we had a baby girl and decided on her name—Kennedy. But the doctor told us that their tests revealed she had Down syndrome. At first, the news was really tough. We both cried, asking, *Why, God? Why us?* News like that, especially when you aren't prepared at all, coupled with the little you know on the subject at the time, just brings out uncertainties and insecurities in most of us. The doctors had told us that abortion was an option, but, of course, that was not at all something we would consider.

Jessica and I began to read up on and learn all we could about Down syndrome. With some education, we no longer viewed this as some sort of tragedy put on us but, rather, a creation of beauty given to us. We accepted the amazing life God was choosing to bring, so we prepared for our daughter's birth.

But on Christmas Eve 2015, Jessica miscarried, and Kennedy entered heaven.

In 2016, we found out we were expecting another baby girl. Yet again, we suffered another miscarriage. The *Why, God?* and *Why us?* questions rushed back in like a flood. But as so often happens in tragedy, we began to meet many couples who had suffered and endured this very difficult trial at various stages of pregnancy. The support is vital because the many unanswered questions and the what-ifs are so hard to manage when your hearts are broken.

But Jessica and I kept believing and trying. In late 2016, we got pregnant again. This time with a boy we named Knox.

One Sunday morning, Jessica woke up and felt like something wasn't right, that something was wrong with the baby. Weary, concerned, and scared for good reason, we both made the assumption that another child was gone. I held her while we cried.

Finally gathering myself, I gently asked Jessica, "Are you positive?"

She answered, "Yes."

Now, I know full well that a woman knows her body, particularly when she is pregnant, so I was not going to question any further. I felt like I needed to go ahead and go to church, so I asked Jessica if she was okay with me being gone for a bit. I needed to hear from the Lord, and being with God's people would be a good place for me for an hour or so. She agreed and I went.

Halfway through the message, I had a strong sense that the Lord spoke to my heart and said these words: *He's still here*. A moment later, I heard, *And* I'm *still here*. There was no mistaking the clarity of the message. By now, I was beginning to understand and distinguish the difference between God's concise and confident voice and my own. I knew that what I heard was not me or my own desires or hopes.

I quietly slipped outside and called Jessica. Cautious but confident, I said, "Jess, Knox is still alive inside you."

She responded, "No, he's not." The thought of me being insistent and potentially insensitive to her feelings, as anyone would understand, began to upset her.

I tried to reassure her. "Hey, this is not me. I believe I heard God speak. I understand the risk I'm taking to tell you this…but Knox is alive."

She paused, then stated, "Wow. You really believe this, don't you?"

I continued, "Jess, I promise. It's not me. I'm telling you right now. I came to church, and I've just been praying. I wouldn't have left in the middle of the service to call you if I wasn't certain the Lord had spoken to me. If I didn't have full confidence in him, I wouldn't dare upset you like this."

Jessica felt encouraged, and the next morning when we went to the doctor, the sonogram gave the evidence of what God had spoken. Our little boy was fine. Perfectly fine. Today, we have two healthy, happy boys, three years apart. And we have two beautiful daughters that we will get to meet one day in heaven.

I Am *Not* My Father

Following all four pregnancies—the two miscarriages and two births—Jessica began to have some health issues. There was even a point where her short-term memory was all but gone. Then her body began shutting down. It was clear her health was failing fast. Even though I had relationships with medical professionals and recommendations for medical care all over the country, we chose to start running a full gamut of tests at a respected hospital in Charlotte.

After all the results came in, the initial diagnosis was chronic fatigue syndrome. Over time, we saw a variety of doctors trying to find a firm conclusion and treatment plan for Jessica to regain her health. One thought it might be Lyme disease. Another tested her for multiple sclerosis—what my mother had suffered from. We couldn't seem to get a definitive answer. Instead, we were told the worst, the opposite of hope. One of the doctors was so convinced that he gave us a book that would teach our boys how to take care of their mom in a wheelchair.

I finally came to the realization that history might be repeating itself. Beautiful wife. Horrible disease. Failing health. Wheelchair. I was about to be put in the exact same position that my father had been.

Upon that strange revelation, I made the conscious and intentional decision that no matter how bad things got, I would *not* take the road my dad did. I would commit. Stay. Remain. Be faithful. I would love and serve, exactly what I had promised Jessica at the altar. I would not—repeat, would not—*become* my father, even if Jessica's health caused her to become just like my mom.

I committed that I would get up early and stay up late to make a living while also making our life work. Every morning, I wrote out a Bible verse for Jessica. I prayed and asked the Lord for the words to encourage her. I kept blocks of my day open so I could get on a call with her or a doctor or leave if I needed to be at home.

On the really tough days, when I wasn't certain what to do, I made one simple choice: do the opposite of what I had seen my father do. I say that with no animosity, but it was simply the strategy that I knew I had to engage at the time.

Finally, the doctors' consensus was an autoimmune illness, meaning any sort of foreign substance or what Jessica's body determined to be toxic, would make her sick. She was ultrasensitive to anything introduced to her system. Through the illness, pain, anxiety, depression, and all that comes with any chronic health issue, we have endured. For her lifeline, Jessica has and does spend a lot of time with the Lord. Today, by God's grace, she has made an amazing comeback and is doing increasingly better. We are grateful to him for answering our prayers.

Jess and I have discovered together that when a crisis arrives, when tragedy strikes, when the unexpected shows up banging at your door, demanding to barge in and disrupt your life, you either surrender to the Lord in deeper ways or you lose faith. No gray areas and no in-between. You pass the test or you don't. You can leave and end up replaying the same behaviors in another marriage with another family like my dad did. And for us, we could repeat the sins of our parents, or we could run to the Father. Decide to break the chains. Change the patterns we were given. Those were the choices. Making the commitment to transform our legacy will never be simple or easy but always worth every effort.

I have heard the story told of how, many years ago, animal trainers in the circus would take a new elephant, usually a baby or adolescent, and wrap a large, heavy chain around the animal's foot and tie it to a massive stake driven into the ground. At first, the elephant would pull and tug against the chain to break free. But the straining to get loose would never work. After a while, the elephant would give up and give in to its state of captivity. As the animal grew to full size, it would eventually stop tugging at the chain. At that point, all the trainer had to do was simply tie a rope to the animal's foot. Because the concept felt the same, the elephant never even tried to escape, believing *anything* tied around its foot held it captive.

This exact style of training from my dad and stepmom worked on me. As a child, I tugged and pulled against the chain. By the time I was in middle and high school, the rope worked. I gave in to the only fate I had ever known. But once I was set free and tasted of the wild—and then was finally set free by Jesus—there *are* no chains large enough to ever hold me now. And from my wife and sons to all my relationships, I only want to be a part of helping people break free from any sort of bondage, spiritual or emotional, by others or self-imposed, from financial to faith issues.

I love when Jesus read from the book (or scroll) of Isaiah, letting everyone know the "me" in the prophecy of 61:1–2 was him!

> The Spirit of the LORD is upon me,
> for he has anointed me to bring Good News to the poor.
> He has sent me to proclaim that captives will be released,
> that the blind will see,
> that the oppressed will be set free,
> and that the time of the LORD's favor has come. (Luke 4:18–19)

6

NO HAVE-TOS, JUST GET-TOS

Now that you know my personal story, heard from Jessica, and learned about our family, I want to go back and draw a parallel line of how my businesses came about. In writing a book, I knew I had to share the personal hardships and struggles from my past so that when I talked about the blessings of my businesses, you could have the proper context before we begin to walk together through the principles I live by.

During my last few years at Tate, prior to launching my own real estate company, I have to confess that I worked way too hard, way too much. I was available to my clients to the point where I was rarely *un*available. I overdid it. Overextended. Overreached. I did *not* have enough boundaries in place between my professional and personal life. I was leaving relational and becoming transactional, out of sheer volume. A lot of people would have called me a workaholic—and likely did.

So I realized if I was going to launch my own company, I would also have to start with the right balance to build a strong foundation. To be a good husband and family man, I had to devote time to being home. As a committed Christ follower, I had to be a good example to the people I hired. With that in mind, I want to begin by sharing a truth with you that I had to learn the hard way:

Trying to be everything to everyone, you end up being nothing to anyone.

This truth is so important that I want to repeat it: trying to be everything to everyone, you end up being nothing to anyone. I realize you may have heard some version of this before, but it doesn't matter who you are, how smart you are, how committed you are, or how you might think you're a cut above others in your industry; this is true for us all. Believing the fallacy that we can "do it all" brings people to divorce or bankruptcy or both every day. Realizing this as soon as possible can save a lot of heartache for you, those you love, and those you employ.

In launching the David Hoffman Group in affiliation with Keller Williams in 2013, I was able to bring along my assistant from Allen Tate Realtors. She worked only for me, so that made sense and affected no one there. I also started with one buyer's agent.

As I brought on more listings, I added more agents. As I added more agents who made more sales, I added support staff. I worked hard to grow while maintaining what we needed to sustain the current business level. It's like balancing scales—when one side tips down, you pay attention to the other side to restore balance. As the money grew, I added a financial person. The upward track was natural and organic. I tried to always anticipate and respond, not react. Anticipation and response are offense, while reaction is defense. If you're only reacting, you're falling behind in the game.

Now, as I share this next season in my company's growth, watch for the success *and* failure. There was most certainly both to learn from. Failure can lead to a downfall, but it can also be growing pains that allow for a major correction to get back on track and be healthy on the other side. Adopting a healthy perspective of the problem is the key difference. The truth of Proverbs is right on once again:

> The road of right living bypasses evil;
>   watch your step and save your life.
> First pride, then the crash—
>   the bigger the ego, the harder the fall.
> It's better to live humbly among the poor
>   than to live it up among the rich and famous.
> (16:17–19 MSG)

Opportunity or Opposition

Because of my success at Tate, coupled with the growth in my own endeavor, I was frequently asked to speak at real estate conferences as well as entrepreneurial and leadership events. I began to find myself in front of crowds in the tens of thousands to tell my story and the power of relationships over rules. At those events, I met a lot of amazing agents around the country. I'm such a major people person, and I can get excited by others' excitement. Some of those conversations began to turn toward partnership and expansion.

I would meet some incredible agent or a team of agents in a metropolitan city. A quick kinship and synergy would occur. In what felt very natural in the moment, an opportunity to go national presented itself. So, in 2014 as a partnership with those agents I had met, I began setting up David Hoffman Group offices around the country.

Once established, I offered them all my resources. I mentored and coached everyone while giving them access to anything or anyone we had available in our home office in Charlotte.

Now, let's fast-forward about three years to 2017 as this pattern and progression continued. I had twenty-five offices around the country. Do the math: that's about one new office every six weeks. At our peak, there were eighty-five agents, and we sold half a billion dollars in properties. To help navigate the endeavor, I had a director of expansion based in Kansas City. *Incredible, right?* Well, it could have been. Just one problem: *me*. (If you're a driven, motivated, high-capacity self-starter, pay close attention now.)

During those three years, I was still speaking at events. I was still involved with my church, charities, and service projects. I was making myself available to all the satellite offices and going to visit them as needed. (Note all the *I*'s.) When I was at home in Charlotte, I wanted to focus on one thing: my family.

So guess what began to suffer? My *own* team back home. The team that I built, alongside Keller Williams, to provide balance for me and the others and the most optimal service for my clients.

What first began to get my attention was that some of my agents and support personnel began to resign. Of course, some of them were normal, natural separations that occur within any company. But some of my team began telling me, "David, we love you, but you're not present. You're not focused. I need to leave and go somewhere stable that concentrates on Charlotte, where *I* sell." (I had obviously violated my own standard number three.) They wanted me to offer more of an intentional plan for how this expansion was going to proceed.

Now, to be fair, the expansion was working at the highest level for others around the country, but I was focusing on relationships *without systems.* You need both relationships *and* systems for a business to be successful, or both will end up failing.

In late 2018, one Sunday after church, Jessica looked at me and stated, "This is going to sound strange to you, I know, but the Lord told me to tell you to stop the expansion. Now, as your wife, I don't want you to stop your speaking. I don't mind you going on the road for a day or two to share the gospel, help people's marriages, or their relationship with Jesus. Even to go talk to people about the value of relationships. *But*...all the offices you've put in are a distraction. They're a distraction from your real estate company here at home. They're a distraction from our marriage and a distraction from our family."

One thing I have learned: when my wife delivers a message like that, I better listen and take action. She never yells. She doesn't demand. She just gives me the truth, firmly with grace. I know she loves me more than anyone and always wants what's best for me. That's her only motivation. I also trust her relationship with the Lord and that she does not take lightly sharing what she hears from him. (Often, when we husbands are not listening to the Lord in an area, he'll tell our wives. So we better listen.)

From the resignations of people I cared deeply about to Jessica's word of warning, I knew I had to take action to correct my missteps. One by one, I contacted each agent in all twenty-five offices and explained the circumstances. I told them I would do anything to help the transition and give them plenty of time to do whatever was needed not to harm their businesses. But, bottom line, I had to create an exit strategy sooner than later. I had to come back home to Charlotte—God's original destination for my success.

Everyone was very understanding, and we worked out the transfer of each agent or team in each office in each city. Some had other options and moved on quickly with no need for my help. I also told them if anyone wanted to relocate to Charlotte, they had a home with us. I don't believe in burning bridges because, most of the time, there are good people standing on them who *will* get hurt in the fire. That makes *exits* just as critical as *entrances*, if not more so. (If you're considering any sort of move or action in your own career, you might want to read those two sentences again—slowly.)

If there is one good thing that came out of that season, it's this: I believe I was able to convert some of those agents from being about the bottom line and making the sale to focusing on people and relationships. I'm not saying anything negative about any of them when we started; it's just the nature of capitalism and the attitude that gets created in commission-based sales. But to work for me, with me, you have to buy into my philosophy on some level. Many of those people today operate their businesses differently because of our time together. If there's any value I added to those agents, it would be the importance of serving and caring about people over and above just making the sale and closing the deal. This overarching principle came out of my background, the adversity I endured constantly offering a powerful perspective. To this day, I am friends and stay in touch with many of those agents.

The moral of this story is that not all growth is good growth. Too much too soon can lead to disaster. What appears to be an incredible opportunity can actually become opposition to your business and your brand.

The worst-case scenario is that you get hurt personally and professionally. While I will always stand behind saying yes, wisdom and discernment are necessary to knowing the timing of whether the answer should be yes, no, or wait. (Wait is actually a great option to practice wisdom.)

Yet again, Solomon nailed it, "Finishing is better than starting. Patience is better than pride" (Ecclesiastes 7:8).

Organic Growth

But *one* failed opportunity shouldn't make us fearful of the *right* opportunities.

Shortly after Jessica's talk with me that day after church, Casey, a good friend and founder of Movement Mortgage, came to me with the concept for a pilot program. At the time, Movement was one of the top-purchase lenders not only in our home base of Charlotte but also across the nation. They were also the mortgage company I had been going to for the majority of my loans for the past thirteen years. The premise of the program was for an agent and loan officer to work next to one another on the same team with the goal of improving communication and creating the best experience possible for both the buyer and borrower. I will never forget what one of their leaders said at the initial meeting about the pilot program: "David, no one wants a mortgage, but almost everyone wants a house. Yet, for the majority of people, the mortgage *has* to come to get the house. So the more we can make the process seamless and offer a circle of trust, the better. A we're-all-in-this-together approach is key."

At the time, the real estate market was really busy, and we had just recently had Knox. Jessica and I were very occupied with life. To counter and contrast my last story, had I gotten scared because of the past or just looked at our current circumstances and said no, I would've missed out on a great opportunity to learn from some of the most amazing, godly leaders in our marketplace, to partner with them on a deep level, growing both our friendship and our business relationship. The majority of the time, saying yes to people whom God places in our lives, whom we respect and who respect us, whom we love and cherish and who love and cherish us is a great idea. Even if it takes a while to see *why* we said yes. Taking one opportunity at a time at face value, doing due diligence, and practicing wisdom and restraint make all the difference.

Digging further into the pilot, one of my agents would call the client, and then the agent would patch in the loan officer. (If you've ever bought a house, you know this is not common procedure at all.) For the clients who would choose us for their mortgage, many of them began to make comments like, "Wow, you all work *together*. This is great." The unique approach helped take the burden off the clients, who, all too often, feel like they have to constantly be the glue of communication between the agent and the loan officer to try to hold the deal together.

What I began to realize as we worked to improve systems and processes during the pilot was that clients who want to buy a house would love for their peace of mind to accompany the transaction. But so much of the buying process actually creates some chaos, some conflict, and can rob people of that peace they want when getting their new home. Too often, a bit of an "every-man-for-himself" attitude can be prevalent when problems arise in a real estate transaction. There can be finger-pointing and some blame game as to why something is or isn't happening. Everyone works to avoid the "one star" ding online for being the weak link in the chain.

After learning what truly worked and didn't work for the client in a true partnership, we discussed a joint venture between a lender and our real estate team. The recommendation for the name was David Hoffman Mortgage to go along with David Hoffman Group, doing business as David Hoffman Realty (DHR). My response was "No, no, no, never again. I don't want my name being the focus of anything else!" I wanted the mortgage company to be about relationships, not me. After all, a trusted relationship was how this all started. Plus, the mortgage company that created the pilot program, as well as the joint venture, did not have anyone's name in its company brand. They were succeeding at the highest level by helping thousands of people with loans and serving even more in need within the community.

In our discussions, we began to talk about the biblical concept of covenant. That word is crucial in both the Old and New Testaments and connected to how we wanted to run our business. After checking into what was legally available, we landed on Covenant First Mortgage. In any covenant relationship—for example, with Jesus or our spouse—the goal is the covenant comes first and should be unbreakable.

By early 2019, with Covenant now being official, we began to pursue the final piece of the real estate trinity, so to speak: the title company. You can have an amazing agent and an incredible mortgage officer, but then the title company can literally keep you from closing on the date you need because of a small detail that someone has missed. To truly offer full service to our clients, the title piece was critical to creating a one-stop shop. A turnkey operation from listing to close, from first look to the final signatures.

We could list, sell, originate the loan, clear the title, and close the deal all under one roof with one team.

Now, of course, there are no obligations for us to serve a client. Someone can choose to use any or all of those three services. We have no problem if someone wants to use just one. But those who do choose the closed-circle approach are often pleasantly surprised, allowing us to take a lot of the stress out of buying or selling a home. *Everyone* is motivated to make the client happy, and accountability is built in.

In 2021, we officially launched Beyond Title. The idea behind the name was to go above and beyond simply checking the boxes on title work. This possibility had been presented to me in 2018, but working hard to be wise about expansion, I knew I had to kick that can down the road for another day. But, three years later, that day finally came, and our business was complete.

A Team Effort

When the pandemic shutdown came in the spring of 2020, needless to say, the real estate business was challenged almost overnight. While online showings were certainly growing and becoming more popular, especially when someone was relocating across the country, the industry and its clients were still accustomed to the norm of face-to-face meetings, driving around to look at properties in person. Now, everyone on our team was at home, working virtually to the best of our ability. We were no longer going into the crowded office for watercooler talk or meetings with a client.

We decided to schedule regular Zoom calls to do all we could to continue our business but also to just stay in touch and encourage one another during such a strange and dark season for the entire planet. We spent time regularly sharing what was going well and what was not. We shared personal struggles. For those who chose to take part, we were even praying together. Our level of serving one another grew exponentially. We had the unforeseen opportunity as a team to laser focus on individuals.

As the interpersonal connections grew stronger among the team, I began receiving emails, text messages, or phone calls from some of them, asking one common question: "What happens after the pandemic ends?"

I finally asked a group of those who had each reached out with this question to meet to talk it over. They offered some logical points to support opening our own brokerage, something I had never imagined doing. Keller Williams had taught me so much and given us so much over the years. We had built our own "Success Team," our name for the admin department. One person pointed out that we were essentially already operating as an independent group in many facets. Their consensus was "David, it won't be easy, and Keller Williams provides a lot for us. But, due to our current organizational structure, we seem to have an even better corporate culture now than before the pandemic."

To be clear, the idea of going independent would never have been an option had it not been for fifteen years with both Allen Tate and then Keller Williams. But, in the summer of 2020, David Hoffman Group went on our own, becoming David Hoffman Realty. At first, we rented temporary space, but then in November of 2021, we were able to locate and upfit our official and permanent office for DHR, Covenant First Mortgage, and Beyond Title. We finally had plenty of room for everyone, along with room for growth. I will always be grateful and never forget the business, real estate, and relationship skills and lessons that I learned from Mr. Tate and Gary Keller, along with the many other great leaders from those companies.

When I did some media interviews to talk about the new company, as is the tendency in this culture, the interviewers asked questions in a certain manner to see if I would offer any disrespect toward Keller Williams. But I didn't. I wouldn't. I have nothing but gratitude and respect for them. Gary Keller will always be a trusted mentor from whom I gleaned so much and learned so many lessons. Plus, I am honored to speak at Keller Williams events, coach Keller Williams team owners, and refer business back and forth across the globe with agents within the Keller Williams network.

Throughout the years, relationships have ruled the day. They have overruled the rules. Movement Mortgage and their joint venture team didn't need me or my real estate company. But they chose us because of the relationships. My friend's wife, who was also an ace loan officer, didn't need to come to work with us, but she did. The attorney friend of mine, who led the setup of the title company, didn't have to help me, but he did.

Moving into 2022, we had fifty incredible agents working with us, all out of the metro-Charlotte area. Today our attrition rate stays at about 5 percent a year. That means that the average agent who leaves does so for personal reasons, such as relocating or retiring. Very few leave to go to another agency. We are a family. We know each other's spouses and children along with everyone's victories and struggles, hills and valleys. We want everyone on our team to win personally and professionally.

Here's the bottom line—the motivation for everything I have shared with you in this chapter—every move I made, even the mistake of the crazy growth with the twenty-five offices, all grew out of relationships. Not building a name, not making more money, not working some ten-year plan, but strengthening relationships. There's certainly nothing wrong with those other things at all. That's just not *my* motivation. The growth I have experienced is from one source—people. Connection. Partnership. Trust. Synergy. No have-tos, just get-tos.

What drives me every day is that I get to serve people in Jesus' name.

To Love, to Be Loved

Because of how much God has loved me throughout my life, I want to be more like Jesus each and every day, a reflection of him, being the hands and feet and showing unconditional love.

> God is love. When we take up permanent residence in a life of love, we live in God and God lives in us. This way, love has the run of the house, becomes at home and mature in us, so that we're free of worry on Judgment Day—our standing in the world is identical with Christ's. There is no room in love for fear. Well-formed love banishes fear. Since fear is crippling, a fearful life—fear of death, fear of judgment—is one not yet fully formed in love.
>
> We, though, are going to love—love and be loved. First we were loved, now we love. He loved us first. (1 John 4:17–19 MSG)

MY PRINCIPLES

For years, I have been sharing the principles I am about to give you. During that time, I've had a lot of people ask me about writing a book. When I felt like the time had come, I had a sense that there needed to be two parts: first, my story. Where we come from provides context for where we are *and* how we got to where we are. Through my story, I want to show that our past does not have to dictate our future. I want to offer encouragement that if I was able to overcome my past, *anyone* can. I also desire to communicate the truth that God created us to experience so much more than this world has to offer.

Principles are simply self-imposed guidelines that are transferable to others. Everything I am about to share, you can do. But your results are your choice. The degree to which you apply them will determine your level of success with each one. As King Solomon stated, "There is nothing new under the sun" (Ecclesiastes 1:9 NIV). I didn't invent these; I just adapted and adopted them for myself. So can you.

One day, I was meeting with one of the agents in my company when the topic of fear came up. Like with any sales position, this issue can arise quite a bit. In that conversation, I made the comment that I no longer have any fear. But something about hearing myself make that statement made me uncomfortable. I knew what I meant. I wasn't scared to risk. To try. To step out in faith. To push the boundaries.

But then I realized I *do* have a fear. A deep-seated fear that, one day, something could go very wrong and I'll be forced to go back to the relational poverty of my childhood. The very worst outcome of that fear would be if I were somehow separated from my wife and sons. I never want to go back to *not* having someone in my life who truly knows me and cares about me. I don't want to wake up one day and *not* have any relationships.

Now, the good thing about my fear is that I don't live to sell houses. Or to run my own company. Or to go give another talk. Or to even write a book. I get up in the morning to accomplish two things: first, to nurture existing relationships and, second, to create new ones. There are many days when I have five meetings scheduled. So you say, *Well, that's to be expected of you, David.* Yes, but here's the plot twist: I have no agenda. The other person may, but I don't. *Why?* Because my goal for any meeting is that I'm just working on a relationship. Can a business deal happen? Certainly. Can a service project be funded or staffed? Sure. Can something in one of my companies get created, expanded, or impacted? Absolutely. But that will be the end, not the means. That will be a by-product, not the product. That will be the result, not the goal. Here's the cool thing: if I end up with just a good hang for an hour at a coffee shop, I feel like the meeting was successful. Because the point was furthering a relationship, making a better connection, or encouraging someone.

Right now, all over the planet, there are people having meetings with one agenda: to get the other person to *do* something. To say yes. To sign the deal. To hand over the money. To agree to whatever the person wants. In fact, the "how-are-yous" and the "tell-me-what's-been-goingons" are just niceties to avoid appearing too direct. So what happens if the person doesn't do what is desired? The meeting was a failure. *Why?* Because the person didn't get what he or she wanted.

But we can *feel* that sense of agenda, can't we? We can read the eyes, the body language, the voice tones, the level of sincerity. Whether we admit it or not, deep down, we *know*. But we put up with it all for the sake of doing business.

Of course, I have no idea where you fall on the agenda scale. But regardless, I want to challenge you to really consider not just reading but also applying these principles. Try them for a week. Two weeks. Fake it till you make it. What if they revolutionize your business? Better yet, your life? Even better, your heart?

7

PRINCIPLE #1

FOCUS ON THE PEOPLE GOD PLACES IN YOUR LIFE

I have found in my own life that the majority of the regrets I have are connected to close relationships where there has been a *lack* of focus. For us all, we have a regret because of something we should have done but didn't. We have a regret about something we did that we shouldn't have done.

In my story, I told you about the events surrounding my mom's death and how my biggest regret was not going to see her when I said I would. Because I never got another chance. The person that God had most prominently placed in my life was my mom. Even though I wasn't with her every day, as she was in New York and I was in DC, she should have been my biggest relational focus at the time. So while "the people God places in your life" typically does mean those in our current physical circles, it doesn't always translate to immediate proximity. This principle has just as much or more to do with emotional and spiritual connection as physical location.

Following my mother's funeral, the guilt, coupled with deep grief and sorrow, created a new relational goal for me: never have a *second* regret.

We are going to have first-time regrets. While we can work hard to avoid them, the goal I'm sharing with you is to not allow a regret to come back around *again*. So you have one, but don't have two. A major way we can battle that dilemma is by focusing on the people God places in our lives. If anyone I love—from a relative to a friend—says to me, "David, I'd really love for us to get together soon," because of my one regret with my mom, I pay attention to that prompt now. I have to consider, *What if this could be the last time I see him or her?* Or *What might God want to do here?* The calling to respond well is not a reaction out of fear as much as a response in faith.

As You Go

Now that we've covered what we can avoid (defense), let's look at how we can engage (offense).

As a Christ follower, I have found that God will place me in people's lives, and others in my life, at strategic times for specific reasons. There are no accidents and no coincidences. Nothing is random. He has a purpose and a plan. We need only to pay attention and obey. Open our eyes, ears, and hearts to where he is at work.

When you meet someone for the first time,

- don't assume that you know what the introduction is about or not about;
- don't dismiss him or her based on any personal biases or judgments;

- don't overlook the opportunity because you are too busy, distracted, or self-focused; and
- don't assume how someone communicates or thinks or what the other person wants or needs.

Create a new habit of offering up a silent prayer, like, *God, how do you want me to serve this person? Show me what you want.* You might be amazed by how God starts to honor and answer those prayers. I know that so many times, I have been amazed by this.

In Matthew 28:19, the Great Commission, Jesus said to "go and make disciples." The implied meaning there is "as we go about life." As we daily live out what God created and ordained us to experience, the natural progression for a Christ follower is to make disciples for him. We live with a new focus and intention. Our part is simply to watch, respond, and obey God regarding those he places in our path.

Let me ask you a question: Who in your sphere of influence right now needs some kind of help?

Go ahead. Think through the list of people around you for whom you could somehow affect or change their circumstances. With something very small or something big but all within your means. That consideration is a game changer and an open door to make disciples and create a real difference.

As a young boy, long before I knew anything about Jesus, I learned to focus on the people around me. Trying to find work to make money throughout the year by mowing, raking, washing, shoveling, all the things I told you I did as a kid, I depended on those I knew and those I could meet within walking distance of my house. Over time, so many people within a mile or so radius, covering many blocks, knew "little David," as I was often called. Neighbors would agree to take a chance on me doing some kind of work for them, and I made new friends.

Had I not been hungry or needy, if I'd not had to make any money or ventured out in my neighborhood to knock on doors, I might never have built my foundation for this valuable principle. Even at such a young age, with no understanding of a spiritual worldview, I had a sense that the people I met were placed in my life for a reason. There was some purpose for knowing them.

Several years ago at a real estate conference, I struck up a conversation with a young man about the concept of job security for an agent. And then, of course, the often-perceived *insecurity* when you're in sales. I shared with him that, to me, the greatest job security any of us can create is not in having an employment contract or a position at a stable company or even a great track record of sales. But rather, we create security by how we focus on the people around us. An others-centered attitude isn't just after the next business deal or transaction or referral or new client but is always seeking opportunities to serve. Transactionally based people tend to roller coaster with the market and economy, while relationally focused people can maintain a steady flow because people needing services from someone they trust is always going to be a reality in any industry.

My friends in Nashville have told me about an unwritten rule inside the music business: "No matter your level of talent, always be a good hang." For example, if an artist is hiring a band to spend the next six months on the road and one player has marginal talent but a pleasant personality with a positive attitude, he or she is going to win out over the incredible player who is known to be a jerk or diva. Artists want people on their tour buses whom they can enjoy being around for the twenty-two hours of the day they *aren't* on the stage. In tight quarters, you're forced to focus on the people around you—positive or negative.

One of the primary aspects of Jesus' mission was to change the world for eternity. Of course, he did, but how? Throughout the Gospels, we see that Jesus invested himself primarily in twelve men and two women. There were the twelve disciples, but also, Mary and Martha seemed to be around quite a bit. There were others in his circles, but as far as the focused investment, there was that same small group. If the Son of God influenced the world with so few, then do we really need a vast network to do what he calls us to do every day? Or do we follow his example by relying on God and focusing on the people he places in our lives? One person at a time, one heart at a time. We don't need *every*body. But we do need those whom God intends to influence us and those we are called to affect.

Jesus' simple sentence in Matthew 6:33 is a fascinating promise: "Seek first his kingdom and his righteousness, and all these things will be given to you as well" (NIV). When you break this verse down, he was essentially saying, "If you will focus on my mission here on earth, I will take care of you here and for eternity. Take care of my kingdom, and I'll take care of your life." Now, look at the next verse: "Therefore do not worry about tomorrow, for tomorrow will worry about itself. Each day has enough trouble of its own" (v. 34 NIV). *Therefore* connects seeking God's kingdom first, today, with the freedom not to worry about what happens tomorrow. What about that mindset is *not* countercultural?

For me, the center of my focus needs to be on the Lord. Next is my wife and two sons. After them, my real estate team and the folks at the mortgage and title companies. Then my current and past clients who may not necessarily need me for anything for years, if at all. With God at the center of our lives, we can then make whomever we are with, the person God places in front of us, our top priority in the moment.

But if I always just move on and never stay in touch with people from past dealings, then that makes everyone just a transaction and not a relationship. We can do an amazing job and serve a client well during the deal, but staying in touch to serve without an agenda is going the extra mile. Focusing on the people themselves, anyone whom God has placed in our lives—even if they can't give us anything—is the right thing to do.

By Jessica and me focusing on the people whom God has placed in our lives, we have been able to have an impact on many. At our home, we've hosted everything from a reception for the governor to baptisms. I've had the privilege of introducing friends to leaders in the state who needed to hear what they had to say. I was able to watch my mother-in-law and other loved ones get baptized in our own backyard. For all these events, we knew whom to invite because we knew their hearts and where they were in life. Because we were current with people, we had a good idea of what they needed and who needed to meet whom for what purpose. Our connections created new relationships for others.

Over the years, I've had the opportunity and the privilege to serve people from all walks of life. I've worked to live by the old saying "Water the grass under your feet." I don't pick and choose people based on age, income, race, gender, or other dividing lines. I choose those whom God places around me whether they love him or hate him. Because I've known what both feel like. I want *him* to choose whom I need to focus on because if I choose, I can mess it up.

God may place people in our lives for a season, for years, or for a lifetime. That's not our call; it's his. And every relationship, no matter how long it's there, is for a reason. We're not supposed to hold on to people whom God intends to be in our lives for a short time, and when things don't go as we thought they should, we don't need to give up on those whom he wants us to serve for years. With God as our focus, wherever we are and whomever we are with can be our priority in the moment.

One simple truth I have seen play out in building my businesses is that no matter the price of real estate or the interest rate or the market or the economy, you can find like-minded, good, caring, considerate, loving, God-honoring people who will work together when the leadership fosters that culture. Which leads me to my next point.

Preserving Your Corporate Culture

For several years, I struggled consistently with an issue. Growing up, as I told you, I never had solid relationships. Once I went into business, when any human I would meet wanted to come to work for me, my response was "Oh, you're a great person. Yes! Come on board!" I was just so grateful that someone wanted to give *me* a chance and wanted to be on *my* team that I felt like no was *never* appropriate. I recall a good friend once telling me, "David, no matter how much success you have, you still seem so surprised when people say yes to you. You realize that you can say no sometimes, right?" But I didn't feel I could or should. While saying yes to everyone is a guaranteed way to build a team, it won't ever be the *right* team, and it won't last.

Once again, I had to look to Jesus. While he specifically called his disciples to follow him, watch what happened when a man he had just set free from demons asked to go with him: "As Jesus was getting into the boat, the man who had been demon possessed begged to go with him. But Jesus said, 'No, go home to your family, and tell them everything the Lord has done for you and how merciful he has been.' So the man started off to visit the Ten Towns of that region and began to proclaim the great things Jesus had done for him; and everyone was amazed at what he told them" (Mark 5:18–20).

The man was filled with excitement and gratitude. He wanted to be on Jesus' team. He couldn't imagine a better place to be. But the Lord understood that everyone in the surrounding area knew the man's history and had witnessed the evil by which he had been possessed. He knew that the best platform for the man to seek the kingdom first was to go show the reality of what God could do. So, in essence, Jesus said, "You're on my team now, but you'll serve me and yourself best if you go tell your story. As you go, I'll see you soon enough." That's the point: What is *best*? *Where* is best?

Several years ago, I came home raving to Jessica about someone I was going to hire. After talking to the person, I couldn't imagine *not* saying yes. (Now remember, Jessica ran a successful staffing business where she connected applicants to employers, seeking the best fit for both.) After hearing me out, she calmly offered, "David, let me guess. They told you everything you wanted to hear. They love your vision. They're going to work with you forever. Everything they said to you was amazing, right?"

I stopped and responded, "Yes, how did you know?"

Jessica continued, "Well, let's think about six months from now. The truth is going to come out. It's like the infatuation phase when you start dating someone. You think you love the person, and everything appears to be perfect. But then you talk about politics and religion and finances and family. You meet the parents. Then it's like 'Wait, who are *you*? Why does everything feel so different now?'"

Then she closed with the toughest question directed not toward the other person but to me as her husband: "Who are you being, and where did the selfless, loyal giver that I married go? The person I met and fell in love with?"

Guilty as charged.

This was exactly why, in Proverbs 31, Solomon wrote, "A wife of noble character who can find? She is worth far more than rubies. Her husband has full confidence in her and lacks nothing of value. She brings him good, not harm, all the days of her life" (vv. 10–12 NIV).

Conversations like this and hard lessons learned led me to create the DHR Culture Committee. This is a team of five people that exists to protect me from myself, from saying yes to someone who will tell me what I want to hear or seeing the excitement as the only factor in hiring someone great. But this committee is also in place to protect the applicant from getting into something that actually does not fit him or her. (If you are a business owner, take note here.)

We don't bring on agents or other support staff simply because they want to come to work for us, have a great track record of sales, or have built a stellar resume. Every year, our Culture Committee says no to more people than they say yes to. Now, I want to be certain you don't think we're being exclusive or elitist or any other negative possibility, especially in our ultrasensitive, victimization-minded society. Let me be clear about our overarching principle. When our team members consider someone, they first want to be certain that we can give *more* to that person than we are going to *take* from the person. We want the person to win, to succeed, and we want to set them up to surpass their three-year plan. The committee's role is to do everything possible to know we can provide that environment.

Another key purpose for the Culture Committee is to ensure that we stay focused on our culture and our character over profit and production.

Applying my three-year plan exercise to this issue, my *plan* was to grow. The *problem* was hiring the wrong people. Bringing in some people who were the wrong fit helped us learn how to know the right ones with the right fit. So the Culture Committee invites the person into the house for a visit but then decides whether it's best for the person *and* our team to come and live there.

There's a strong likelihood that you have worked with enough people to have been a part of an incredible team. There's also a good chance you have worked with a toxic group. But too often, what happens is that just one wrong person can bring toxicity to a great team. The old agricultural saying "One bad apple can spoil the whole bunch" is very true for teams of people and actually happens too often in the workplace.

Does this dynamic always mean the person is bad? Of course not. What can happen is that he or she is not the right fit or comes to the realization that he or she is not happy in the setting. That dynamic, when left unchecked, can start to breed discontent, negativity, and eventually a poisoning of the entire organization. The ripening to rotting process starts and slowly affects everyone, even those who were 100 percent happy before.

Today, in my own company, there are quite a few people whom I don't meet until the Culture Committee has approved and hired them. I trust that team implicitly, so I believe whomever they bring on is the right fit for us and us for them.

From a spiritual standpoint, our company has Christians of different denominations, Jews, agnostics, and atheists. But they all love each other. We focus on what brings us together, not what could divide us. It's really beautiful. Our society screams and preaches diversity, but what is diversity worth without love? The culture of our team is diverse *and* loving. Everyone watches out for everyone else and has each other's backs. Professionally and personally.

One of our team members, Angela, has a son with mental health issues whom she and her husband wanted to homeschool. But she also wanted to continue her career. Balance was her need. Because Angela fits our culture well, we've worked hard to accommodate her family's needs. In her own words, she shared, "Working with DHR allows me the gift of being able to best serve my son. I have a business that flexes with my schedule and my family's needs. They have supported me in every way. David's coaching, coupled with Katherine's training, has propelled me to have more business than I ever had at past companies, all while meeting our family's needs. Experiencing crises is always tough, but knowing you have a team who loves you and is rooting for you to win in every aspect of your life means everything."

Another team member, Bettina, who also works with our nonprofit Hope to Home, shared, "Working for DHR offers me a tremendous opportunity to expand what I once thought would not be possible for me professionally. David has an innate ability to see and encourage each person's gifts and talents. We are provided the support to run in freedom to be the best we can be, the best for the team, and the best for our clients."

These are testimonies to the incredible work of our Culture Committee and our entire team's ability to focus on the people around them, regardless of what they believe spiritually.

Let's close this principle with our action points, some of which are repeated from earlier, to focus on the people God places in your life:

- You may have a regret, but don't have a second one.
- The best job security can come through having an others-focused attitude.
- No matter your level of talent, always be a good hang.
- Focus on people even when there's nothing for you to gain.
- Whether someone is in our lives for a season, years, or a lifetime is God's call.
- Before someone comes on your team, be sure you can give him or her more than you will take.
- Fit is more important than a yes or no.
- When you meet someone for the first time,
    - ◊ don't assume that you know what the introduction is about or not about;
    - ◊ don't dismiss him or her based on any personal biases or judgments;
    - ◊ don't overlook the opportunity because you are busy, distracted, or self-focused; and

◊ don't assume how someone communicates or thinks or what the other person wants or needs.

APPLICATION EXERCISE

List your concentric circles of relationships of everyone around you right now, starting in the middle with those who are the closest in your life.

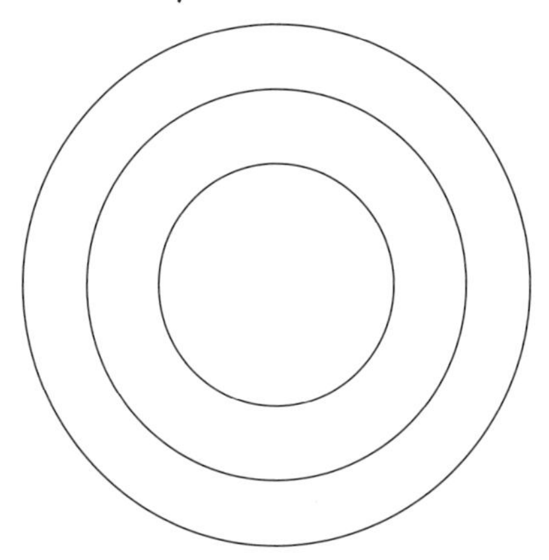

Who in your life right now has the greatest influence on you? Explain.

Who in your life right now can you help in any way?

Do you view those in your circles as more transactional or relational? Explain.

What can you do to improve the culture of your work environment?

What is one simple, practical step you can take today to focus more on the people God has placed around you?

Who in your close circles might feel like you are not there for them?

Have you been present with each and every person whom God has placed in your life right now?

Who has not heard from you in the past thirty days whom you should have contacted?

In what percentage of your relationships do you work to give more than you take? Explain.

Who in your life needs a prayer? Who needs a celebration?

8

PRINCIPLE #2

SPEND TIME WITH OTHERS WITHOUT HAVING AN AGENDA

In the 1954 classic film *White Christmas*, Rosemary Clooney's character confesses to Bing Crosby's character that her sister wrote a letter to him pretending it was from their brother, Bing's old army buddy. Bing smiles and says, "You don't have to apologize. Everybody's got an angle."

To which she responds, "That's a pretty cynical point of view."

Bing, in his trademark swagger, states, "Come, come now. Surely you know that everybody's got a little larceny operating in them. Didn't you know that?" Bing's character, a seasoned entertainer, didn't seem offended at all. In fact, he'd grown accustomed to everyone "working an angle." But the integrity of Clooney's character was offended by his tainted response.[3] This conflict among humans, depicted well in this movie scene, is as old as sin itself.

Today, we live in a culture in which cynicism, suspicion, skepticism, distrust, doubt, and sarcasm are increasingly the order of the day. It starts to feel like everyone suspects that everyone else has an angle to work—"a little larceny"—to steal something personal: resources, money, time, energy, or attention. That toxic attitude is contagious and easily creates a constant defensive stance even in Christ followers. In fact, in too many instances, the Western church has been as guilty of perpetuating this as the marketplace. (And we're supposed to know better.)

Yet, we can only be responsible for our own attitudes and actions. Personally, I have found the best way to proactively counter the culture is to try to engage the three action steps below. I'll personalize the statements and questions by presenting them in the first person.

1. In your relationships, identify your own potential agenda or angle.
    - What am I really wanting to get or give here?
    - Am I consciously wanting to receive something?
    - Am I subconsciously after something?
    - Am I focused on taking or giving?
    - Do I care about the relationship or just the transaction?
    - If the person knew my real intent, would he or she still be interested in the transaction?
2. Once you recognize it, remove that agenda from the table.
    - Why do I think I need this person to do something for me?

- How can I achieve the same goal by giving and serving instead?
- How can I turn this into a win-win for everyone?
- How can I honor God and others with an alternative goal?

3. Focus on the person or people.

- How can I turn the focus from "what I want" to "what they need"?
- How can I turn "what's in it for me" to "what's in it for them"?
- Where is there an opportunity to serve?
- How might God want to use me in the person's life?

Bottom line: whatever *you* may want, flip the circumstances to see what the *other* person needs.

As Christ followers, we have to remind ourselves daily that if we follow his lead, we must also adopt and engage his mindset and lifestyle. Think like Jesus and act like Jesus. For many, the following passage might have become too familiar, but we have to allow the truth of the Word to keep refreshing and renewing our minds and hearts. Regardless, let the power of these words sink in: "Jesus called them together and said, 'You know that the rulers in this world lord it over their people, and officials flaunt their authority over those under them. But among you it will be different. Whoever wants to be a leader among you must be your servant, and whoever wants to be first among you must be the slave of everyone else. For even the Son of Man came not to be served but to serve others and to give his life as a ransom for many'" (Mark 10:42–45).

So "lording over" people to flaunt and misuse authority is, of course, not a new concept. From the time the first person became a king or queen or any nation's equivalent, we've had this issue. That's why Jesus' counsel is as timely today as it was the day he delivered it. Yet being a servant leader seems to be a conflicting idea to many people, causing questions like, "How can you possibly lead while also serving?" "How do you serve people if you're out front leading?" and "How can you keep moving forward while helping others in their journey?" I want to help answer these questions, or at least the spirit of these questions, in the presentation of this principle.

Here's one encouraging alternative to the culture: Serving people is what we were *all* put on this earth to do. Our careers just become a great way to do that. I'll repeat that statement, and I hope you let it sink in deep: Serving people is what we were *all* put on this earth to do. Our careers just become a great way to do that. The service is the "what." The career is the "how." Yet isn't it fascinating that the world teaches us that we are to work our way into the position of having *everyone* serve *us*? The concept of success has been twisted just like everything else that God intended to be good.

I'm going to spend the bulk of the chapter on this principle offering you examples of how it played out when I *re*focused my focus on spending time with people without an agenda.

Interaction after the Transaction

To share this story while protecting the person's identity, I realized that describing him as "a prominent businessman with a great family" is honestly a huge part of my client base. I'm grateful I can say that. So, with one particular friend who falls under that description, three months prior, we had sold his house and helped him find and buy a new home. I was a bit surprised, and a little embarrassed, when I realized ninety days had passed without me contacting him again. Knowing he most likely wouldn't need my real estate services for a very long time, I reached out and said, "Hey, I can't believe it's already been three months since we closed, but I wanted to see if you'd want to get together and catch up. Maybe have breakfast some morning?"

He soon responded, "Thanks, David. I'd love to get together," and we set up a morning to meet. Because he also knew I couldn't possibly be connecting for business, he showed up with his guard down. After we small-talked a bit and ordered breakfast, I asked him about his family. Quickly, this linebacker-sized man's man had tears welling up in his eyes.

He gazed down at the table and responded, "David, I knew you were going to ask about my family, and I decided that I was going to be honest with you. Because of my place in the community and all the people around me, I haven't known whom I could talk to, whom I can trust, who might judge me, or whom I might negatively influence. We're in a dark place. It's not good. I'm sleeping in another room. I may have to leave soon. I'm brokenhearted about where we are."

He kept opening up, in and out of letting some tears fall while fighting others back. Surprised by his confession while also beginning to realize why God had placed him on my heart, I asked the usual questions: "Has there been an affair?" "Is there still an affair?" and "What happened?"

He answered, "No, nothing like that. Neither of us has been unfaithful. I honestly am not even sure how things got *this* bad."

Over the next three hours, we talked in-depth. After he finished, I shared some of my own struggles, failures, and regrets. As the conversation grew more transparent, he began to realize his intense focus on work was the likely catalyst for the issues. And, of course, I understood the constant battle for that balance. His job had become his first priority over his marriage and family—an all-too-common cancer that can consume someone and is also often difficult to admit, much less start to fix. But as he spoke, some light began to slip through the cracks and enter the dark place. I could see the change in his countenance. A little hope began to show in his eyes.

I encouraged him to do whatever it took to set things right, to believe that it was not too late. There was time to get honest with his wife and work out the issues. I assured him that he could replace his job but not his family. The big realization in these crossroads moments is that the mistakes don't have to lead to *more* mistakes. Change is possible and available. You may have a huge wound, but you have to try to stop the bleeding.

At the end of our time together, he was resolute about going home to begin the reconciliation process, sharing, "David, I didn't feel like I could just reach out to anyone, even my quote-unquote *friends*, especially the ones who are in strong marriages. I couldn't tell them that I'm about to leave my house. Because then I feel like I become a bad influence on them. If their wives don't really know me, then they might not want their husbands around me. I don't want to be 'that guy.' I didn't feel like I could be vulnerable to just anyone. So when you reached out, I knew you didn't have an agenda. I really appreciate you allowing me to just be me and be honest, no matter how bad it is."

Especially for someone trying to live a Christ-centered life, I hope you are starting to see the futility of making ourselves available only when we think we might make some money or because someone is influential or might do something for us. That's a one-dimensional life.

Spending versus Investing

I will never forget speaking to a large group of real estate agents in Baltimore a few years back. At the end of my talk on the value of relationships and serving people, I allowed some time for a Q and A. I saw a hand go up in the back of the room. When the mic runner handed him the mic for the audience to hear his question, the man asked, "Mr. Hoffman, what if all you do is focus on helping people"—making air quotes with his fingers when he said "helping people"—"but no one ever buys a house from you, and no one ever asks you to sell their home?" I could tell by the guy's attitude that he was actually making more of a sarcastic statement than asking a question. He didn't want an answer; he just wanted to say that he didn't buy my talk. Which is certainly his prerogative. I think that's one of the reasons Jesus so often said, "Anyone with ears to hear should listen and understand" (Matthew 11:15, among others).

Reading the man's demeanor, I responded, "Well, that sounds awesome. Because when I get to heaven, my goal is to hear Jesus say, 'Well done, my good and faithful servant,' because he didn't leave me on earth between salvation and eternity just to make deals but to help people. If my biggest problem is I've helped *too many* people but none of them bought homes from me, well, I guess my calling wasn't to be a marketplace ambassador as much as to serve people at a higher and deeper level, even more than working in real estate."

Now, let me say, I get it. I knew where the guy was coming from. We all have to make a living, right? I have a lot of salespeople and entrepreneurs tell-slash-ask me, "I don't know where to spend my time. If I have a meeting and nothing comes from it, then that's one less meeting I can have with someone else." Time is such a valuable commodity, and our time really does translate to money made or money lost. That's why a lot of us in the marketplace live with a constant level of anxiety about where to most productively spend our time. So we must all make a choice for each hour of every day, and we have to live with that choice. But just like I did for that guy in Baltimore, I'm only offering you my choice as an *option*.

We must realize there is a difference between spending time and investing time. Is spending better than investing or vice versa? Just like with money, the answer depends on the circumstances. But there are things we spend time on that we will never see any benefit from, while there are other things in which we invest our time that yield a massive return. An extra hour a week with each of your kids. A two-hour block of no interruptions or distractions each week with your spouse. A meeting with your core team every Monday. In those examples, you aren't spending but investing.

I know a lot of what I am sharing is countercultural, but Jesus, the One I follow, was the most countercultural figure in history. *And still is*—just try bringing up his name in conversation. On the one hand, relying on God for his provision as we serve people is really a simple way to live, to say, "Okay, God placed this person in my life right now, so I'm going to do my best to be there, however I can." On the other, it's so easy for us to be torn and spend so much of our days living out King Solomon's frustrations that he shared in Ecclesiastes 1:14: "I observed everything going on under the sun, and really, it is all meaningless—like chasing the wind." But focusing on the people God has placed in our lives can actually give life meaning and make life much easier to navigate.

Whether in Solomon's day or ours, we can combat and counter this "chasing the wind" with the goal of trying to touch as many people in our circles as possible within a thirty-day window. Some kind of touch twelve times a year, if at all possible. A simple text, a phone call, an email, or a handwritten note, depending on the circumstances and connection. Now, while that may be a simple approach, it is not easy at all. If we have a lot of people in our database, especially those outside our close friend circle, it can feel a bit overwhelming at first. But, for years, that has been my goal, which keeps me proactive, not reactive, in my relationships.

Now, let's bring this concept back around to my client friend in the breakfast meeting. The biggest takeaway from that story, and this entire principle really, is had I not reached out to him with no agenda, could he have gotten things turned around for him and his family some other way? Well, yes, of course. But those three hours became the divine appointment that God used to help him. I simply had to be available and willing. I just had to ask him how his family was doing and listen. He did the heavy lifting from there because he was ready. He only needed an opportunity.

But my friend wasn't going to post his problem on social media. He wasn't going to raise his hand, even at his church, and say, "Hey, everybody, I'm in a really bad place. My marriage is failing. Help!" Someone had to reach out and simply ask the right question, offer a listening ear, and lend a helping hand with nothing to gain. *Me* having no agenda allowed *him* to set the agenda.

This principle has a secondary aspect that always points the finger back at me and causes me to reflect on my own life and make adjustments where I need to. After meeting with him, I had to ask myself, *Is there anything I need to examine in my own family and my own focus on business? How am I doing in that area?* Every opportunity to serve also becomes a teaching and evaluation pit stop for our own lives.

Sovereign Circumstances

In 2014, a friend of mine, Ben, told me about his friend, Jimmy, who was working toward getting into real estate. Ben asked if I would be open to meeting with Jimmy to share some guidance about how to succeed in real estate as a new agent.

Ben told me that Jimmy was working on acquiring his license. So I knew that there was no guarantee he would even get into the industry. Jimmy was also a popular local deejay, so he already knew a lot of people in the realty business. Because of his thriving career as a deejay, I figured real estate would not be his top priority. For those reasons, I assumed the odds were actually against us ever working together. But, because of my friendship with Ben, I agreed to meet Jimmy for lunch, knowing I would help him out however I could.

After sitting down and small-talking for only a few minutes, we quickly connected.

Shortly after that first meeting, Jimmy did get his real estate license, which allowed me to make him an offer to come to work with our team. He hit the ground running, getting off to such a strong start that, within a few years, he became a coach to our new agents in our hub office in Charlotte and at all the other satellites I had around the country at that time. Jimmy continued to deejay for our own client events as well as many of the fundraisers we held at my home. While he wore many hats in business, throughout his life, Jimmy put a smile on the face of each and every person he would ever meet.

Fast-forward to 2018, I was speaking at a real estate conference in Nashville, Tennessee. The host had asked Jessica if she would secretly get a half dozen friends and colleagues to share some encouraging words in letters about what their relationship with me had meant to them. At the end of my talk, the host gave the letters to me, one of which was this note from Jimmy:

> David—
>
> You are an amazing person. So glad that we got introduced. You have helped me in so many ways. The biggest not even being my business. You have led me back to find my faith. I lost faith years ago as I struggled through a divorce, through an addiction, and through depression. But as I healed, I would look to you and see your faith and see your passion for God. I started to look back and see my faith wasn't lost, just misplaced. You never gave up. You kept asking and telling me about Jesus and God. My faith is coming back to the forefront of my life, my family, and my heart! And you are the one I need to thank for that!
>
> Love you like a brother!
> Jimmy

Four years later, in early March of 2022, a senseless act of violence outside his home sent a stray bullet traveling through the window and striking Jimmy while he was with his wife and daughter. He died almost instantly. Later that spring, I came upon his letter to me. After rereading it out loud, I fell to my knees, sobbing and missing Jimmy here on earth while also being eternally grateful for the fact that he knew and loved Jesus.

The Midwife Ministry

I want to offer an analogy to drive home this unique role of connecting God and the people he wants us to serve. The practice of having a midwife to assist a mother has experienced a resurgence as a viable option for giving birth. A midwife helps the process along, works to avoid complications, ministers to the mother, and assists the baby during the birth. Let's say you're at someone's home where a midwife is in another room with a delivering mother. Suddenly you hear the baby cry, and next you hear those in the room expressing their joy at seeing a beautiful child come into the world. What you would never expect is for the midwife to walk out of the room holding the child and announce, "Look, everyone! I made a baby!" If this did happen, you would immediately try to get the infant away from the midwife as quickly as possible. *Why?* Because making such a statement would be crazy. The midwife cannot take credit for the conception, the pregnancy, the birth, or the baby. The role is merely to assist and help bring about the best result.

Daily, in bringing God's will to the earth, those of us who follow Christ are essentially midwives. He is continually bringing people to an understanding of who he is through the Holy Spirit (spiritual conception). He allows us to be involved in the process of him bringing people into his kingdom (new birth). While we cannot take any credit for the conception, the process, or the delivery, God chooses to use us to be an instrument to assist and bring about the best result, to do everything possible to see his work completed in the lives of those around us. Then, once we have assisted the Father—taken part in the ministry of a midwife—he will look at us and say, "Well done, good and faithful servant."

Let's close this principle with some action points for serving without an agenda.

- Lead by example without words, as in, "Watch me, then follow my lead."
- Always give more than you take, even when someone else is giving.
- Teach yourself to pay attention to people. See everyone, even those whom others think are invisible.
- Keep the focus on the other person or people.
- In your relationships, learn as much as you can about where the other people are in their lives. Learn their successes. Learn their challenges.
- Don't assume anything about anyone. Find out for yourself.

APPLICATION EXERCISE

On any given day, do you tend to be cynical or hopeful in your approach to people? Why?

Think of a current situation involved with your business where you engaged with someone. Why did you initially reach out?

Once you reached out and spoke, did you follow up? If not, why not?

Who *hasn't* heard from you this month who should have? What has caused you to avoid or delay reaching out?

If a transaction occurred, have you been in touch *outside* of the deal?

What is one upcoming appointment on your calendar that you could turn the tables from selling to serving?

From what past transaction could you reach out to someone with no agenda?

How might God want to involve you in his work to allow for his agenda instead of your own?

9

PRINCIPLE #3
FIND A WAY TO SAY YES

Today, we all know we're surrounded with nos, negativity, and naysayers. All news seems to be bad news. We read it, hear it, see it, and feel it. Without anything to combat this spiraling social paradigm, we can become skeptical, cynical, and distrusting. Maybe you realize you've fallen prey to this attitude. "They" have gotten to you. You tried but couldn't beat 'em. So you gave in and joined 'em. You don't like it, you didn't plan it, but it's where you ended up. Or maybe you're standing on the brink at the edge of optimism, looking for any form of inspiration not to go over to the dark side. You're holding on by a thread, holding out hope. *Believe me, I get it.*

Yet, wherever you find yourself today on the scale from hopeful to hopeless, let's look at finding a way to create positivity in our lives. Not a denial of reality or a stick-your-head-in-the-sand move, but an intentional decision to work at bringing out the best in all circumstances. As you clearly know by now, I had to constantly fight back my past to make that choice in my present. I had to consistently choose to find a way to say yes. And hear the yes. To change my life and the lives of those with whom I have the privilege of working.

As I also told you in my story, I heard *no* from my earliest memories until my self-proclaimed emancipation from my stepmother as a young adult. After that, I vowed that I would live my life working to do two things:

1. Give the yes
2. Get the yes

Adopting number one is crucial, but I want to encourage you to also adopt number two. Depending on our personality, we can often feel like other people deserve the yes but we don't. Or the reverse, we feel we always deserve the yes and don't think about giving the yes to others. This principle works best in a bundle, as a package deal. It's a circle, not a straight line. *Why?* Well, here's a story Jesus told for you:

> Therefore, the Kingdom of Heaven can be compared to a king who decided to bring his accounts up to date with servants who had borrowed money from him. In the process, one of his debtors was brought in who owed him millions of dollars. He couldn't pay, so his master ordered that he be sold—along with his wife, his children, and everything he owned—to pay the debt.
>
> But the man fell down before his master and begged him, "Please, be patient with me, and I will pay it all." Then his master was filled with pity for him, and he released him and forgave his debt.
>
> But when the man left the king, he went to a fellow servant who owed him a few thousand

> dollars. He grabbed him by the throat and demanded instant payment.
>
> His fellow servant fell down before him and begged for a little more time. "Be patient with me, and I will pay it," he pleaded. But his creditor wouldn't wait. He had the man arrested and put in prison until the debt could be paid in full.
>
> When some of the other servants saw this, they were very upset. They went to the king and told him everything that had happened. Then the king called in the man he had forgiven and said, "You evil servant! I forgave you that tremendous debt because you pleaded with me. Shouldn't you have mercy on your fellow servant, just as I had mercy on you?" Then the angry king sent the man to prison to be tortured until he had paid his entire debt. (Matthew 18:23–34)

Regardless of how you feel about Jesus and the Bible, this parable rings true then and now. We see this paradigm happen in the human race all the time in big and small ways. Here's a simple, everyday example: You see a guy in jammed-up traffic working hard to get other drivers to let him into the lane. Finally, someone backs off and allows him a gap to ease in. He *gets* the yes. Then you watch as he guards his new position to not allow *anyone* in ahead of him. He refuses to *give* the yes. What went around is not going to come around on his watch! Here's what you can bet if you see someone make that move: he doesn't just act like that in traffic; it's a lifestyle. Getting the yes but not giving the yes.

A midlevel manager figures out how to pad his paycheck by justifying to his boss several hours of overtime each week, all while cracking down on his team to work harder but stay at forty hours for his numbers to look good. A department head who is single regularly comes in late and leaves early but gives her people grief when their children get sick and they need to go home. A CEO refuses year-end bonuses to the company after being told by the board of directors the amount of bonus he will receive. Every day, at epidemic levels, people want to be forgiven for millions while they collect their thousand, just like in Jesus' story. Or in the Western culture today, they refuse the thousand for others while collecting their million.

But then there are the ones who give a yes *and* get a yes. That's who I want to be. That's who we should all strive to be.

Become a Yes Hero

In 2000, Sara Blakely took a hard-earned and harder-saved $5,000 and started her own company built around an idea she had for a new undergarment for women. When she told people that her goal was to one day reach the $20 million mark, they laughed at her exuberance. Her mission for her company name and product, Spanx, was to deliver "amazing products to women to use their very feminine principles in a very masculine space."[4]

In 2012 at the age of forty-one, Sara became the youngest woman to make Forbes Magazine's list of billionaires with no inheritance or other help. In 2013, she became the first female billionaire to sign the Giving Pledge, a list of wealthy people vowing to give most of their fortune to philanthropic causes.

Then in October of 2021, Sara sold a majority stake in her company for $1.2 billion. *Yes, with a* b.

Sara *got* a huge yes, but then she decided to *give* a major yes to her employees. She announced that each one would receive two first-class round-trip tickets to anywhere in the world *and* $10,000 to pay for the rest of the trip.[5]

Could Sara have just announced the massive deal, and everyone would have been happy for their founder and boss? Sure. But she wanted to reward the people who had risked with her and helped build her business into a billion-dollar company. She did not just get the yes, but she gave the yes.

Sara Blakely is a "Yes Hero" because when she received the yes, she gave the yes. That's when *everyone* can win. But no one won bigger than Sara, from her investment account to her generosity bank. (Can you imagine how much fun and joy she had announcing the gift to her employees? And then imagine all the incredible stories she heard as they returned home and shared the adventures she provided.)

So how can *you* become a Yes Hero?

First, we have to understand that it's not about the amount of money or the size of the opportunity but about looking for ways to say yes and bless others. The benefits of proactively seeking out how you can find the yes in your life—to both give and receive—will offer a far more positive perspective as well as create a rewarding and satisfying life in all respects. The guy in my hypothetical traffic example gave us a snapshot of his selfish, me-first lifestyle. In real life, Sara gave us a look at who she is as a person and business owner. A Yes Hero is not created overnight but in the small decisions that eventually build up to the big ones.

In our personal lives, this principle can be applied as well. For example, with my family, if Jessica asks me to assemble something she has bought for the house, it's easy for me to think about being tired or how much time I *don't* have. But if I answer, "Yes, I can do it, but what's your time frame? When do you need it done?" she may reply, "Oh, just sometime this next weekend is fine." Then I've said yes to my wife, and I can now plan for the task. Find the yes and then quantify the expectation.

The same is true with my sons. Consider if one of them says, "Hey, Dad, we want to play ball in the yard." Instead of saying, "I don't have time right now," I can say, "Okay, can you guys give me a half hour to finish up what I'm doing?" or "I can't today, but let's play tomorrow before dinner." Again, find the yes and quantify.

Be a Yes Hero everywhere you can in every role you are in.

The Extra-Mile Mindset

In the days of Jesus, a Roman soldier was able to demand that a Jewish citizen carry his pack for one mile. Refusal could be met with a beating or worse. The common response was to begrudgingly grab the pack, watch the path, and at exactly one mile, drop it, and run. Fulfill only the letter of the law to avoid punishment. So when Jesus told the people in Matthew 5:41–42, "If a soldier demands that you carry his gear for a mile, carry it two miles. Give to those who ask, and don't turn away from those who want to borrow," the directive brought some culture shock. Basically, he said, paraphrasing, "Fulfill the law by carrying the one, but then, to honor God, go *another* mile. Maybe even tell the soldier why you're walking on with him." The yes is not in the first mile because it's presumed and assumed. The yes is in the *extra* mile.

In our respective careers, we all quickly learn the "one-mile rules"—the stuff you gotta do. The minimum things that are expected. The baseline. Then sometimes the game changes, and we find out the expectation has changed and that something new has been added. A simple example is many years ago, when you ate at a restaurant of any sort, sodas cost per glass or cup. That was the rule. You want a second one; you pay for a second one.

In the late eighties to early nineties, the paradigm slowly changed to free refills while you're at the table. In 1988, Taco Bell called the move a part of their "value initiative."[6] Before long, customers began to ask, "Do you have free refills?" For many people, if the answer was no, the customer would say, "Then I'll just have water." Eventually, the desire to sell soda made what was once the second mile become the first mile. Free refills became the norm. Today, the extra mile is asking, "Would you like a refill to take with you in a to-go cup?" The one-mile and second-mile dynamics happen all the time in the marketplace. We would do well to pay attention to them and stay ahead of the curve.

Consider these questions:

- Are you still in the first mile even after your industry adopted an extra mile? Is the lack of a yes costing you?
- What might be your next value initiative that goes past the industry norm, a way to give a yes that helps people and maybe even create a pleasant surprise?
- How can you identify more yeses in your career?

The Yes Heroes work to give a yes, assuming the first mile, then finding and going the second. The extra mile becomes second nature. Let me repeat that—the extra mile becomes second nature.

Saying Yes for the Big Picture

I have always had anxiety when it comes to flying—the takeoffs, the landings, and especially the turbulence. But I don't get on planes and endure my fear of flying because I love traveling. I get through flights by focusing on the fact that I will meet new people at a real estate conference or at a speaking engagement or make memories on our family vacation. I don't fly because of business *or* pleasure. I say yes to flying because of one thing: *relationships*. That perspective change turns my "I'm really dreading that business trip next week" into "I'm really looking forward to meeting new friends and helping my old friends."

On one particular trip, a veteran flight attendant noticed my pale-white knuckles putting a death grip on the armrests of my seat. She quietly asked me, "Son, do you believe in God?"

I immediately responded with a "Yes, absolutely, I do."

She smiled and politely said, "Well, today may be *your* day to go to heaven, but do you think it's time for *all* 165 of us to go?"

She so got me. I laughed and let up my grip on the seat. But that flight was my vehicle to some new relationships.

Another time, an older woman seated beside me began to ask questions, starting with "Do you fly a lot?"

I answered, "Yes, a good bit."

Obviously seeing my discomfort, she continued, "Well, if you hate it this much, why do you fly so much?"

I thought to myself, *She asked, so I'm going to be honest with her.* "My boss tells me to travel."

The lady kept going. "Oh, what do you do for a living?"

I responded, "I'm in real estate."

A little surprised at my answer because most real estate agents sell only in the city where they live, she asked, "Mind if I ask who your boss is?"

"No, I don't mind. It's Jesus. He wants me to travel so I can share the good news about him. And I also teach people how to focus on the relationships in their lives. How if God is in the center, then whoever you're with can be first." *I don't think she saw that coming.*

Of course, none of us can, nor should we, always say yes. Nos are necessary in life. But we could all use a little more yes, right?

Because we live in a fallen state in a lost world, conflicts are going to arise because we have to say no when someone wants a yes. Or maybe we said yes to one person and someone else didn't like it. Because of these constant circumstances, we must quickly say yes to the opportunity to

- resolve an issue,
- reconcile a circumstance, or
- reach out and extend forgiveness.

A wise man once said, "A great gauge of our spiritual maturity is the length of time between the offense toward us and our forgiveness of it." One of the pillars of a strong team, and something we work hard to live out at David Hoffman Realty, is to be quick to resolve any sort of conflict. Saying yes builds a good offense and a great defense. Commitment to these kinds of disciplines is what creates authentic relationships.

The Most Personal Yes

In my life, the most important yes I ever gave or got was my decision to stop living life my way and give my life to Christ. After dealing with everything I shared with you about my childhood up through my twenties, I was ready to live life in a new and different way. The gospel just made sense to me.

While I am certainly no evangelist, I never want to miss an opportunity to offer someone else his or her yes for Christ. That's why I believe it's important not only to be able to share about Jesus but to know when and how as well. Jesus ministered to people as individuals, according to their need, so we must follow his example. Depending on whom I'm talking with, I will share different perspectives of who Jesus is to me. If the person has little knowledge of Christ, then I talk about the journey of the Son of God, from a baby who came humbly in a manger through his thirty-three years up to his death on the cross.

I have found that one of the biggest questions people have about Jesus is that if he was God, why would he stay on the cross until death? All while he had the power to do whatever he wanted and come down? For me, I have arrived at the place of believing that God's plan required three more days to complete the mission, so he had to see it through. He stayed on the cross *because* he was the Son of God. We humans would have done everything to save ourselves. Exactly the reason we need salvation!

I have had discussions with many nonbelievers and those who are staunchly opposed to giving Jesus any credit. When you unpack all the details of his death and resurrection, there's a lot there that can't be humanly explained. The empty tomb is a historical fact. Yet if even an atheist is willing to entertain the conversation, I freely say, "Look, if I'm completely wrong about his deity, then at least I'm living my life more and more like a Man who was such a great example of how to live and lead. How could you find a better role model?"

On the argument that Jesus was some sort of crazy man, my answer is why would a liar, a con man, wash the hands and feet of his disciples, even the one who betrayed him? Still today that is considered one of the greatest acts of humility a person can do for another. In the garden of Gethsemane, when Jesus asked his Father God if there was any other way to redeem humanity, he realized he had to die a brutal death for our sins. But he also knew about his resurrection because he spoke of it many times. So I believe that everything he has done for us all provides the proof, without a shadow of a doubt, that he is who he said he was.

When I have people ask me why I don't seem to struggle with fear or why I don't get completely stressed out or worried in a crisis, my answer is that everything has already been done for us by Jesus. If we believe he's got us, the worst thing that can happen is death, and death means going to heaven, which is a beautiful thing. That's why the focus of my life is becoming more like Jesus, growing closer to him in a personal relationship. He has given me the authority and the opportunity to live *like* him on this side and *be* with him on the other side. That, my friends, is the beauty of the gospel and the point of faith.

One of the greatest things I love about Jesus is how he loves unconditionally, forgives easily, and gives continuously without ever receiving anything. Once again, who could be a better example? In my marriage, fatherhood, friendships, and business relationships, my goal is to be like Jesus: to not keep score, to focus on giving and not on receiving, to concentrate on loving and not hurting, to remove any idols and the things of this world, and to keep my eyes on him and his Word. If Jesus was able to forgive Peter after Peter betrayed him three times, if Jesus was able to wash Judas' feet at the Last Supper, then I can forgive too. I often say that in all aspects of my life, I fail every single day because I am a sinner, but when anything good comes from me, that is Jesus.

Even the greatest skeptic can agree that Jesus *did* live how we all *should* live.

We know the bad news because we hear it every day—this world is getting a lot worse than we ever imagined. But the gospel—the good news—is the work of salvation that has already been done for us, so we don't have to worry about trying on our own but simply trust in him. And second, if we know Jesus as our Lord and Savior, this life may get worse. But heaven will be so much *better* than even our best day here.

Because Christ is the central focus of my life, I wanted to commit some time in this principle of saying yes to share a little about my faith. I hope and pray that you would say yes to Jesus for the first time or for the last time if you already knew him but have gotten offtrack. The gospel is available to everyone. I close this section with a few very foundational verses for a relationship with Christ.

- "We are made right with God by placing our faith in Jesus Christ. And this is true for everyone who believes, no matter who we are. For everyone has sinned; we all fall short of God's glorious standard. Yet God, in his grace, freely makes us right in his sight. He did this through Christ Jesus when he freed us from the penalty for our sins" (Romans 3:22–24).
- "God showed his great love for us by sending Christ to die for us while we were still sinners" (Romans 5:8).

- "The wages of sin is death, but the free gift of God is eternal life through Christ Jesus our Lord" (Romans 6:23).
- "If you openly declare that Jesus is Lord and believe in your heart that God raised him from the dead, you will be saved. For it is by believing in your heart that you are made right with God, and it is by openly declaring your faith that you are saved" (Romans 10:9–10).
- "Everyone who calls on the name of the LORD will be saved" (Romans 10:13).

Let's wrap up this principle with some action points to give the yes and go the extra mile:

- As you are in the midst of a project, sale, or transaction, look for ways you can go above and beyond and give more than you receive, even to the point of taking a loss.
- Always watch for how you can help someone else win.
- Don't just do the minimum to check the box or finish your commitment but push yourself to your true potential. That's the only way to stretch your limits and grow.
- Do just as much to give, to help people, when *no one* is watching as you would when *everyone* is watching.
- Give even when you won't get any credit.
- Always test yourself on how you set your personal limits as to what standard is acceptable to you. Give 100 percent in any situation, even if less is expected or accepted by others.

- Give as much *outside* of the transaction as you do *inside* the transaction.

To be sure you apply this chapter, I want to invite you to take a few minutes to evaluate your own ability to get a yes and give a yes. The more you put into these answers, the more you will be able to apply the truth in your life. Be honest with yourself. Dig deep and think big.

APPLICATION EXERCISE

Do you believe you tend to say yes more than no? Explain your answer.

If you tend to say no, what typically drives your reasoning? *Why* do you tend to say no?

Do you enjoy giving a yes, or do you struggle with it? Explain your answer.

Regardless of your previous answers, what would you have to change to say yes more often?

How might giving more yeses improve your life?

What is one simple, practical step you can take today to become a Yes Hero and adopt the second-mile mindset?

10

PRINCIPLE #4
YOUR PAST DOESN'T HAVE TO DICTATE YOUR POTENTIAL

When you were in the middle of my story, if you had stopped reading there, what *potential* might you have thought I'd have? Becoming a young man angry at the world? Prison in my future? Poisoned with hatred and bitterness? A cynical adult who's out for everything he can get for himself? Yeah, totally possible. In fact, the odds were stacked far more on that side of the scales. Just applying my childhood story to simple statistics would tell the tale that I was headed for trouble.

As a young man, did I have the opportunity to repeat the sins of my father? Absolutely. Once again, statistics would skew toward me doing just that. Yet, today, while Jessica and I don't claim to have a perfect marriage, we do have a strong marriage. And we are committed parents to our two boys. Just because those things happened to me as a child did not mean my future was, or is, doomed to repeat the past. God has given me my own free will and my own choice to not repeat my father's life but to repent and turn those tragedies around to create the *opposite outcome*.

Around the time I got to middle school, somewhere deep inside, I gathered up the determination that I would somehow one day change the life I had been handed. I would be different from my father. My past would not—repeat, *not*—dictate my future or my potential to succeed in life, relationships, and career. And then when I met Christ at almost thirty years old, all the dots began to connect. I realized the life that God had designed for me all along, no matter my circumstances growing up. His redemption changed everything and offered me a clean slate driven by *his* potential, no longer my own as a victim of my upbringing.

My life makes no sense, but it was never in my hands or my parents', always in my Father's hands. The world screams loudly that our past determines our future. But God whispers to us that our past does *not* dictate our potential. Jesus died for all—regardless of our past—so that we can experience new life.

> Since we believe that Christ died for all, we also believe that we have all died to our old life. He died for everyone so that those who receive his new life will no longer live for themselves. Instead, they will live for Christ, who died and was raised for them.
>
> So we have stopped evaluating others from a human point of view. At one time we thought of Christ merely from a human point of view. How differently we know him now! This means that anyone who belongs to Christ has become a new person. The old life is gone; a new life has begun! (2 Corinthians 5:14–17)

Whatever your story, good or bad, divine or dysfunctional, *you* are no exception. Your past does not have to define your potential or your future. Age, gender, race, background, family history, bad breaks, and bad choices, along with any and all dividing lines in humanity, don't have to create any limits when we follow in our Father's footsteps.

When I moved to Charlotte, most people would have thought that it would have been impossible for me to sell forty-plus homes in my first year in business. *Why?* Because I knew no one. While I could have used that as a roadblock, it actually ended up being a blessing. Also, since I didn't know very much yet about Charlotte, I was able to spend the majority of my time becoming "the expert." I dedicated my days to showing any properties I could, having coffee with anyone and everyone whom God placed in my life—potential clients, new friends, and even agents who were supposed to be "competition." I spent nights on my laptop doing research, working to discover a good deal versus a bad deal, along with due diligence as to what different demographics of people were seeking when they looked for a new home.

I learned as much as I could about the many different areas, suburbs, neighborhoods, and streets. I educated myself on the school system and the school districts. I learned what people wanted in a home and community. Because time was on my side and I had no history with anyone, I had the freedom to learn. And I did. I took advantage of my abundance of hours to create an edge for when my relationships began to form. The best analogy I can offer as to my viewpoint and approach in those early days is an Olympian training hard, getting ready for the games.

Once I began to connect with potential clients, I had a clean slate and could earn the relationship. I freely shared my knowledge and proved my value. Not knowing anyone as "the friend," I was able to lead as "the expert." No one knew me as "John and Jane's son," "a guy I went to high school with," or even the server at their favorite restaurant who's trying to get started in real estate. There was no backstory to add to or overcome. I was new—a fresh face and a fresh voice.

I have always loved to be the friend first. It's a lot more fun and actually easier. But we have to go with the season we're in at the time. Learning Charlotte, I was able to become the trusted adviser and real estate agent of choice. Through that expertise and working hard to be present with my first-time clients, I was able to build lasting relationships.

When I read the Gospels through this filter, I wonder if some of the disciples' struggle with Jesus' true identity was because he became friends with them first. Especially in the beginning, they didn't look at him as the expert, even though they witnessed him heal and perform miracles. The challenge for them was *How could our friend Jesus be the Son of God?*

> When Jesus came to the region of Caesarea Philippi, he asked his disciples, "Who do people say that the Son of Man is?"
>
> "Well," they replied, "some say John the Baptist, some say Elijah, and others say Jeremiah or one of the other prophets."
>
> Then he asked them, "But who do you say I am?" (Matthew 16:13–15)

The turning point came when Peter spoke up: "You are the Messiah, the Son of the living God" (v. 16).

Because of his revelation and transition regarding Christ's divine mission, Jesus was able to reveal Peter's true identity to him. Peter's past would no longer dictate his potential.

> Jesus replied, "You are blessed, Simon son of John, because my Father in heaven has revealed this to you. You did not learn this from any human being. Now I say to you that you are Peter (which means 'rock'), and upon this rock I will build my church, and all the powers of hell will not conquer it." (vv. 17–18)

Defying the Odds

One of the major issues that we must keep working to solve in this country is the many areas where the culture actually works to keep kids from experiencing their full potential. As affluent as much of Charlotte, North Carolina, is, we are no exception to having deeply impoverished areas. Few careers highlight those differences more than being a real estate agent, as you direct people to where they want to live and where they should avoid. That's just the nature of the business. But for me, that puts a greater responsibility on me to try to be part of the solution and not perpetuate the problem.

In 2013, I was on the board of directors for the foundation of a Carolina Panthers player who served at-risk youth in Charlotte. When he got traded to the Giants, the move understandably affected his ability to focus on our city. But having seen the kids who live in poverty right under our noses, I felt a burden to find a way to keep serving them. I felt called to try to make a difference in this area. Just like me as a child, the kids in those neighborhoods have no choice in where and how they must live their lives. One day, they'll each make their choices about their potential and futures, but for now, they must try to survive.

Another nonprofit that did similar work threw out an idea to me. They wanted to re-create in a local middle school a program that they had started in Raleigh. The leadership asked if I would go into Martin Luther King Middle School and set up an after-school program to teach sixth, seventh, and eighth graders about real estate. At that time, the majority of the kids at the school lived in households below the poverty line. Most were fatherless with a single mom working all the time, trying to pay the bills.

Because of my love for my mother, I have always had a soft spot for single moms and their children. As a kid, when I would visit my mother, I didn't realize how hard it was on her to have her only child taken away and not be able to see me more than four or five times a year. While I always saw my mom's smile, I had no idea the hurt that she must have been feeling. For those reasons, I love giving single moms an opportunity to become agents in our company.

When I met the principal, she told me, "When the kids start pushing back, that's when you need to know that you're getting through to them. It's just a defense mechanism because they're told, directly and indirectly, that they're not allowed to be smart and try to succeed. If they're showing up, then they're paying attention to what you're saying. And they're a lot smarter than they may come across."

Being a voluntary program for the students, the nonprofit had secured a teacher who agreed to offer her classroom. She would sit in the back during the sessions to represent the school and deal with any issues since she knew all the kids. I jumped at the chance to lead the effort.

On the first day, we had twenty students, divided evenly between boys and girls. To get to know them, I asked questions about their goals, hopes, and dreams. The consensus of the guys was they all wanted to be LeBron James, and the ladies wanted to be Beyoncé. I did my best to encourage them by explaining that there was only going to be one LeBron and one Beyoncé and that they needed to become who God created them to be. My biggest goal was to inspire each one to be the best he or she could be and to let them know that God had a plan for good for each one of them.

I shared a little bit about my own childhood while making it clear I didn't have the same childhood, just a *different* version. Hunger is hunger. Loneliness is loneliness. Being told you can't is the same message, no matter your age or ethnicity or color or neighborhood. I told them, "I'm not comparing my life to yours, but I am saying I can relate. I have some idea of what you're going through."

I continued, "I cannot imagine what each of you goes through when you leave here each day. I know some of you may be struggling and hurting. But I want you to know that when I moved to Charlotte years ago, I only owned what I had in my car, and I didn't know anyone. My mom had died, and my father was not in my life. I had no idea if I could make it in real estate, but I knew I had to try. But today, some of my clients are your sports heroes that you want to be like. That's because God can place people in your life no matter what career you have." I also challenged them to consider how they could help the people who live in their neighborhoods and even in their own families.

While I may have lived in a somewhat middle-class home, *my* life was definitely well below the poverty line. I shared with them that if I could have a purpose, they have a purpose. When I was in the seventh grade, I had no idea there was a plan for my life, but the good news is that I was there to tell them there was a plan for theirs. I didn't know God at their age, but I was there to tell them they could. To fulfill what I was there to teach, I told them how they could become a real estate agent and even how their moms could be an agent. The goal of the program was to give them hope and show that even though they're not going to be Beyoncé or LeBron, that doesn't mean that they can't have an incredible, successful life.

On day one, they showed me their minds—both sides of their brains. In that first class, I saw how smart they were on the left side. Then on the right side, they showed me how big of a vision they had as they answered all my questions.

One particular young lady whom I'll call Chloe was so bright and so creative. She wanted to learn and had real talent. She and her mom were homeless and went from shelter to shelter. But her mom made sure Chloe was in school every day. During the first two weeks, Chloe was very creative, imaginative, and visionary. She was smart and paid attention.

But before the third class started, the teacher pulled me aside and said, "Hey, I just want to warn you that Chloe's getting bullied for being in this class. Word is getting around that she's answering questions and that she's smart. So I'm just preparing you that it might be rough with her today. She still wants to be here, but she has to change the narrative out there to survive."

I was devastated that the peer pressure was actually working against the kids, making it harder for them to excel and grow, the very reason I was there.

Sure enough, when class started, Chloe turned on the attitude. She cursed at me and acted like she didn't care. While I knew the truth that this was all an act, it still broke my heart. I also found out that when she left class to walk home, she was being threatened with getting beat up if she didn't quit. All for just trying to find a way to a potential path out of poverty.

One of the young men I'll call Andre was so smart, talented, and obviously loved to learn too. On the first day, he quickly expressed an intense interest in real estate. As we began the second class, I realized he wasn't there. Afterward, I asked the sponsoring teacher, "Hey, do you know where Andre is?"

She gave a deep sigh and answered, "Yes, I do. He's grounded from being here."

Shocked, I responded, "Wait a minute. Let me get this straight. This after-school program to help him possibly find a path forward and a bright future, that's designed to give him hope and keep him off the streets, *that's* what his mom took away from him? Not a cell phone or TV time but *this*?"

The teacher said, "Yeah, David, I felt like crying when I found out. Because he told me he loved the first class and couldn't wait for the next one. But evidently, when he went home and told his mom how much he loved it, she came back with 'Great, well, you just lost it because you didn't listen to me and clean your room.'"

His mom grounded him from the class for a month. But, fortunately, four weeks later, he returned and completed the course.

I discovered quickly, just like the principal had warned me, that in their preteen world, anyone who is deemed to be smart is not cool. A lot of the kids were bullied and taunted for participating in the course. After a while, the threats got to some of the kids, and they began to be rude or aggressive with me and the sponsoring teacher. But I found it interesting that they would always show up while trying to prove to the other kids they were not going to allow us in. What struck me was seeing that these kids had internal and external discouragement coming at them.

But the investment in all twenty of those kids paid off. For our last day, I asked every student to prepare a visual presentation with a brief talk on what they had learned in the class. We got permission to have the event in the school auditorium and allowed them to invite family members. Every student had at least one person there—moms, grandmas, and aunts. Unfortunately, not many men. We had food afterward and made it as special as we could.

For Chloe's presentation, she had a large canvas with cut-out pictures of different types of real estate—a farm, condo, mansion, single-family home, tract of land, and even a warehouse to represent commercial real estate. She talked through the various uses for each property. Chloe proved to everyone that her future was going to be as bright as she could possibly choose it to be. I sat by her mother, who cried as she watched her daughter on the stage. Her pride and joy as a single mom created such a great moment in validating the entire effort.

My experience there was a roller coaster of ups and downs. But in the end, I was so proud *of* them and *for* them. I was also grateful for each one and excited for their futures. I prayed that my words of encouragement would pop into their minds and hearts to remind them of God's yes when life told them no.

When you grow up seeing some of the worst in humanity, you don't scare as easily. Yet, I also learned a long time ago that you can never fully understand what a person is going through. You need to recognize that someone is hurting, that someone is struggling, but don't tell them you understand. Because you don't, no matter how similar it may be to your circumstances, it's never exactly the same.

I wasn't spared the bullying during my time at the school either. On one class day, I stopped to get gas close to the school. Some guy called out, "Hey, man, you're in the wrong part of town."

I smiled and answered back, "No, sir, I'm exactly where the Lord wants me."

Surprised, he yelled, "What?"

I continued, "Yeah, I'm going to go where I'm supposed to be today. I'm about to go teach about real estate right there at the school." I pointed as I finished.

Obviously taken aback, he walked over to me. "Really? What do you do there?"

We ended up having a great conversation. The key is to not be scared of people and places that are different from what we are used to. There are no gray areas when it comes to comfort zones. We're either in them or out of them.

Allowing the past to not dictate potential can manifest in more than one way. I want to share another story where someone was successful in one career but was forced to make a change. So many of us think for years that we are a one-trick pony, but then circumstances or opportunities challenge us to realize we have more to offer. Choosing your potential is not always going from bad to good; it may mean we need to make a choice from good to best.

One-Way Trip to Charlotte

In May of 2020, my dear friend Josh reached out and said, "Hey, one of my best friends in California, Jon, is looking to move to Charlotte. He's a great guy. Do you have any openings at your real estate company?"

I answered with my usual response, "Well, we always have room for a good person." Then I clarified, "He'll have to get licensed."

Josh got more specific. "I think he's going to need a steady income."

I said, "Okay, maybe on our mortgage side?" I promised Josh I would check on the possibility and get back to him.

What I didn't yet know was the reason why Jon and his family were wanting to leave San Diego from his job of being a worship leader at a large church. In 2013, he was diagnosed with a brain tumor that almost took his life. While he survived, the tragedy left him deaf in one ear, taking away his ability to sing at the level he needed to lead worship. But now, a major factor was the horrible pain he suffered associated with the tumor.

After Jon had started his recovery, he and his family had come to visit Josh and his family. While in Charlotte, he realized that the humidity dramatically decreased his pain. He said that it virtually went away after a few days here, but when he returned to Southern California, it came back. He figured out that climate was a key factor in managing his pain. In this new season, Jon felt called to leave church ministry and join the marketplace, believing that as long as he followed the Lord, he could make a difference anywhere.

Now, a lot of people would say, "Let me get this straight. You think a worship pastor from San Diego,

California, is going to be a successful loan officer in Charlotte, North Carolina?" My reasoning was that, bottom line, the guy knew how to build authentic relationships.

When I went to my mortgage partners and presented Jon's story, they responded, "Have you met this guy?"

I said no.

They continued, "There's no way, David. He doesn't know anyone here. He's never done a loan before. He doesn't check a single box for the job. Mortgage needs attention to detail, even more so than real estate. Coming from a creative world in music, not only does he not have any experience in this business, but he's also artistic, creative. This is all analytics. It's numbers, and you can't afford to mess them up. No, it won't work." They closed with "Why do *you* think this will work?"

"Well, I say yes because I love Josh, and any friend of his is a friend of mine. I trust him as a dear brother, and I believe it's going to work."

They pressed harder. "We've done this longer than you. As your partners, why can't you just trust us?"

I responded, "Look, guys, I get it. I understand your concerns. I do. And I do trust you. But I trust the Lord that he had Josh ask me to help Jon."

A final pushback came. "David, it's not going to work."

Trying to be diplomatic but direct, I added, "Anyone who can be a worship leader at a big church, travel the world, and be bold in his faith is going to be really strong in relationships. Stop saying no; just say yes, and I'll pay every dollar for him until we can see how he does."

Finally, they said, "All right, Dave, you know what? We're going to say yes. Because we trust you. And if it doesn't work, there's going be a lesson here."

Knowing Jon's salary was the biggest concern with our business being so young, I offered to front his first year from money outside the mortgage company. That way, if it didn't work, my business partners wouldn't be affected, and I would be the only one hurt in the deal. If it did work, then the money would work out and make sense moving forward. But they even agreed to work with me on the money as well.

I called Josh and told him. Grateful, he asked, "Well, don't you want to meet him first?"

I smiled and said, "I want to talk to him, but no, I don't have to meet him first."

Now, I know you're wondering, just like my business partners, why would I take the risk and agree to this when I didn't really know Jon? The answer is a relationship. Josh is one of my most trusted and closest friends. He has rarely ever come to me with things like this, so when he did, I knew I had to help. I believed in Josh's belief in Jon.

So Jon and his family moved to Charlotte, and they jumped right into the community. He and his family joined our church. Soon, I saw him walking around talking to people on Sundays like he's been here longer than I have! Everyone loves him. He's becoming a marketplace ambassador for Christ. He's growing and learning. His pain is managed, and his health is good.

If one day Jon leaves Charlotte, if he doesn't stay in mortgage or he doesn't stay with us, the bottom line is he allowed God to take a life-threatening and life-altering obstacle and turn it into an opportunity to serve God in a completely different way. What a great testimony we were all able to be a part of! And as for Jon, he still serves the same God. He still has the same mission. His assignment just changed. His past did not dictate his potential.

One day, I asked Josh, "How does Jon already know so many people?"

He answered, "He just genuinely knows how to *meet* people." Then he added, "Thank you for offering the opportunity when we needed it."

Regardless of your past, whether you relate to my story, the story of the kids at Martin Luther King Middle School, or Jon's story, we are all having to constantly work to eliminate things in our lives that hold us back from being all God created us to be. Sometimes we get stuck, for months or years or even decades. But the takeaway from this principle is that it is never too late to change until we breathe our last breath. The God of redemption is always ready to take us to new places through his transformation.

With that closing thought, the application section for this principle is designed to help you navigate where you've been, where you are, and where you need to go.

APPLICATION EXERCISE

Think about your own past.

What odds were stacked against you that you had to overcome?

What stats could have told a different story for you?

What specific roadblocks and obstacles have you had to overcome?

What in your past has *not* held you back from you reaching your potential?

Now, think about your future.

Is there anything or anyone in your past who is still stopping you from being all you were created to be?

Is there anyone or anything who has told you there is something you cannot do or something you cannot achieve, and have you allowed that to limit your potential?

Is there anything that is causing you to feel a no toward your dream and your destiny, and you need help to get rid of it and move on with your best life? Explain.

Write out a plan of action, addressing your answers to the previous questions. What steps can you take? What actions do you need to implement right away? How can you be sure your past no longer dictates your potential in *any* way?

11

PRINCIPLE #5
ADVERSITY CAN CREATE GRATITUDE

One Halloween night when I was in elementary school, my stepmom took my sister and me around the neighborhood to trick-or-treat. Coming back home, as we turned the corner onto our street, we saw some boys out in front of our house. As we got closer, I could tell it was a group of my buddies from school. Maybe they had come by to see if I could make another round with them? But as we got closer, I realized that was not the case. They were throwing eggs at our front door. As my stepmom began yelling at them to stop, I saw that every kid was one of my "friends," and the ringleader was the guy I called my best friend.

I'm sure you're thinking, *With friends like that, who needs enemies?* Yeah, growing up, it was not cool to be my friend. I was one of the "weird kids." Even if I considered someone a friend, that didn't necessarily mean that the sentiment was returned. And sometimes, whether the other guys would admit to being my friend or swear they weren't depended on the level of peer pressure in the room at the moment. That's a snapshot from my childhood memory album I will never forget. Whether a bully was ten years old or forty, the adversity of navigating those kinds of challenges was constant for me.

When I share my story at conferences, conventions, churches, and other events, I always talk about how adversity created gratitude in my life. Quite often, after I speak, I have people come up to me and ask, "David, how in the world can you say you're grateful for such a horrible history?" People struggle to understand and tend to think that such a mindset is somehow illogical, maybe even unreasonable or out of touch.

The short and simple answer is that *because* of all that adversity, I grew from a boy into a man who, still today, is grateful for the basics, like a good meal and access to clean water. My childhood is so burned into my brain and heart that no matter how many blessings God gives me, I remain thankful for the little things, the simple things in life. The truth of Ephesians 3:20 has certainly been personalized for me in that God has done "immeasurably more than all [I] ask or imagine" (NIV). This single truth is a major part of my life message and why this principle is so important to me.

While painful memories can certainly torture us, they can also create a constant stream of gratitude for what so many people have come to expect, feel entitled to, or take for granted. All while most of the world is just trying to survive each day. We must somehow keep in mind that those who don't live in the first world don't live like we do. We have problems like the barista screwing up our latte or the Wi-Fi glitching during a Zoom call. To offer some perspective, there's an old Haitian proverb that says, "A rich man is one who goes to bed knowing he has food for tomorrow." As hard as it may be to understand with a suburban utopia mentality, we all have to remember the truth that there are people in our own cities struggling with hunger, just as I did, regardless of how or why.

Some of what I'll share in this paragraph is a repeat, but my mom was such an incredible example to me of being grateful. Throughout my growing up, she was my only real role model. She taught me gratitude more from her example than anything she ever said. First, she seemed thankful to just be alive. As I've mentioned, she always had a smile on her face when I saw her and always spoke highly of her friends and family. On those last few calls, I had no idea if she knew how sick she was because she never once complained. Amazingly, in my twenty-four years with her, I didn't hear her speak anything negative about my father leaving her and taking me. My mother also never said a word about the sacrifice she made to bring me into the world—unlike my dad and stepmom, who used it as a weapon. The picture I have in my mind of my mom is her beautiful, beaming smile. My life has been changed because I know Christ, but my heart is grateful because of my mom. She is the reason for this chapter.

Prison or Palace

When I look at the Bible and think of who best represents this principle, Joseph from the Old Testament stands out. But his childhood was completely the opposite of mine. He was the golden child in his family. He was "Daddy's favorite," so much so that his older brothers hated him. The infamous coat of many colors that, centuries later, spawned a Broadway musical was a symbol of favoritism and the family's dysfunction. Joseph's hardships began around the time mine started to subside. We both got free from our families, but that's when my life began to have hope. However, that's when Joseph's took a severe nosedive. But the very point of Christianity is that God is the God of the mountaintops *and* the valleys.

Taken from Genesis 37 and 39–41, here's the highlight reel from Joseph's life:

- He was the favored son of his father from among all the brothers.
- His father gave him a very special coat that became the last straw for his brothers.
- His jealous brothers decided to get rid of him.
- They stripped him of his coat and sold him to traders as a slave.
- They told their father that Joseph was killed by a wild animal, using the shredded coat as evidence.
- After being taken to Egypt, Joseph was sold as a slave to Potiphar, an official of Pharaoh.
- Potiphar soon placed Joseph in charge of his entire household.
- Potiphar's wife attempted to seduce Joseph.
- Joseph refused her, and she accused him of attempted rape.
- Joseph was sentenced to prison for many years.
- Pharaoh heard that Joseph had successfully interpreted dreams and called for him.
- After interpreting Pharaoh's dreams and implementing a God-inspired plan to save the nation, Joseph was made second-in-command.
- Joseph's brothers came to him and appealed for help, even though, now that Joseph was an adult, they had no idea who he was.

- Joseph was eventually restored to his family after he saved them from a famine.

Happy ending? Well, yes, but from the time of his brothers' betrayal to his promotion in Pharaoh's palace, these events spanned from around the time Joseph was seventeen years old to when he was thirty! He spent his last few teenage years and all of his twenties in slavery or in prison.

Here's the connection to our principle: regardless of the ups and downs in Joseph's life, in Genesis 39:2, we find that "the LORD was with Joseph, so he succeeded in everything he did." In verse 23, we see a slightly different version: "The LORD was with him and caused everything he did to succeed."

Now, I realize this doesn't say anything about Joseph's level of gratitude, but we have to take the entire context of Scripture to heart here. Throughout the Bible, do we ever see God bless and show favor to anyone who has a bad attitude? An ungrateful spirit? An entitled posture? No. In fact, those choices often caused people to miss God completely—like Jonah, Job's friends, Saul, Judas, Ananias, and Sapphira, for example. So we have to know that the entire time Joseph was enslaved or incarcerated, he served and loved the people around him, all the while believing God would take care of him.

Joseph never had a choice in what was happening to him, but he always had a choice in how he responded to it all. *Just like me, just like you.* When he could have gotten bitter and decided to live as a victim of his brothers' evil, instead, he maintained his character and integrity. Think about how different Joseph's life might have been had he chosen to hate his family and everyone who harmed him, including Pharoah. In his high position, he even had full authority to take revenge on his family, but he chose instead to forgive them, bless them, and take care of them. Ironically, that set off the chain of events that fulfilled the very dreams he had shared with his family years before, back at home, that fueled the hatred of his brothers.

In Joseph's story, we see that God's definition of success has little to do with wealth or position and everything to do with character and faith. Whether in the prison or the palace, no matter where God placed Joseph, he was always the same man of faith.

So, as both a maturity test and a reality check for us all, we must ask ourselves the following:

- Do I celebrate when everything is going great but complain with every crisis or downturn?
- Does my attitude operate on a sliding scale, fully dependent on my circumstances in the moment?
- Is my life lived in moods, where people are never quite sure who I'm going to be?
- Am I good with God when he blesses, but do I doubt him when he seems to be silent?
- Do I view my current status in life as his blessing or curse, reward or punishment?

There is a massive lesson for us all to learn from the life of Joseph, which is likely the very reason God placed the story so early in his Word. I mentioned before how my life was in the opposite order of Joseph's, yet the great news is that both of us ended up in blessed positions, only and all because of the God we serve. The same is available to you and can be true for your life as well. Romans 2:10–11 states, "There will be glory and honor and peace from

God for all who do good—for the Jew first and also for the Gentile. For God does not show favoritism."

Championing Perspective, Changing Perception

The perspective I carried into adulthood was that no matter how bad things got, life could always be so much worse. Because it had been! As I entered a career in real estate, that attitude of humility motivated me to help people whom other agents didn't want to bother with. But, as a result, someone whom I helped find a cheap rental house later turned into a first-time home buyer. Then a few years down the road, after landing the dream job, he decided to sell and buy his dream home. Then he told his parents to call me when they decided to move to the area. You never know how just being grateful for the chance to serve someone whom others ignore can keep multiplying opportunities over many years.

A small sale years ago where I worked hard to serve the client eventually turned into an opportunity to help an entire company relocate. I've had friends for whom I helped buy their starter house refer me to Carolina Panther players looking for multimillion-dollar homes. Then that referral turned into my helping other teammates. Being faithful in little can lead to God opening the door for all kinds of relationships. But that faithfulness is most always born out of gratitude that came from adversity. Even in 2008 and 2009, when being a real estate agent was not a popular career, I still had the perspective that it could be so much worse while remaining grateful for all that I still had in my relationships.

Leaving Joseph's story as well as mine, let's turn these thoughts toward you.

Whatever has happened to you in your own life can create the choice and the opportunity for a new and fresh perspective for which to be thankful. While it's actually easy for adversity to make any of us bitter and cynical, turning the tables on our perception can lead us to be grateful for *any* good that comes into our lives. This is exactly why a very common response for someone who has been brought back from death's door is to be so grateful for life like never before and to have a brand-new appreciation for living. Most become grateful for their next breath when they realize they almost breathed their last.

If you have never had any real adversity in your life yet, that is certainly not your fault. And no one wants to sign up for trouble. But, understandably, you likely won't have the perspective of how bad things could actually be. That, in turn, also means you might not be grateful for how *good* things can be either. If that is true, then take it from me, be very grateful for your lack of adversity!

The older I get and the more success I experience, the more I see that my greatest asset and resource is my gratitude for every relationship. Here's one example of what I mean. A friend of mine was diagnosed with a form of blood cancer. Through that experience, I got involved in the local leukemia and lymphoma foundation fundraisers. After two years of service, the foundation asked me to join the board of trustees. On that board, I made friends with a financial adviser for many pro athletes. He connected them to me whenever they needed a real estate agent. What began as a concern to serve a friend and merely help a cause progressed into a series of introductions I would never have made otherwise. In fact, I would go so far as to say that had

I tried to get in front of those pro athletes without those connections, they likely would not have given me the time of day because those people are so accustomed to everyone trying to get to their money somehow.

Now, as I share stories like this, I want to be crystal clear. I never—and I repeat, never—go into any relationship or setting because I think I'm going to get something out of it. Motive is crucial here. What I am saying is that when we work to serve and build relationships, God will honor that obedience and take care of us when the time comes. I echo back to when I previously shared Matthew 6:33 to again express that powerful truth from Jesus: "Seek the Kingdom of God above all else, and live righteously, and he will give you everything you need."

I truly believe that my struggles growing up have always driven my motivation and inspiration to serve in my community. But I also believe that is what drove me to strive to accomplish so much as a young adult. One example is, in 2009, when I began serving at the Charlotte Junior Chamber, also known as the Charlotte Jaycees. My mentor, Mr. Tate, along with a good friend, suggested I get involved in the organization. So, trusting those relationships and recommendations, I went all in, even though the economy had bottomed out. I helped wherever there was a need, giving my time.

I also started telling everyone about the group—friends, clients, and colleagues. My obvious passion and excitement led to us bringing on over one hundred new members in my first year with the Junior Chamber. Through our concerted efforts, we built a library in Kenya, started a citywide recycling drive, and brought in some high-profile leaders, such as the governor, mayor, and local CEOs, to speak encouragement and inspiration to young businesspeople. We were also able to secure some celebrities and artists, like Sugar Ray, to perform at our fundraisers, taking in hundreds of thousands of dollars for local causes. During that season, our chapter became one of the fastest growing in the country. From that, I ended up being elected president, the same position Mr. Tate had held fifty years prior. I was grateful to have the opportunity to continue in his legacy and walk in his footsteps, which was always a privilege.

The way I see it, my adversity led to a different perspective, that new perspective led to gratitude, gratitude led to service, service led to opportunities, and opportunities led to growth. Don't most of us change more from having to deal with our burdens than from our blessings? Don't we tend to mature the most in the battle in the valley than in the celebration on the mountaintop? So much of how we change is because we realize we *have* to before we will *choose* to.

Hope to Home

The apprentice-style program I previously shared with you that I had helped start at Martin Luther King Middle School had become the catalyst for my desire to serve those struggling in our economy who just needed to be given a break. Back in Principle #4, I talked about my friendship with Josh, a pastor at our church. One day as he and I were talking about our shared burden for the city, I said to him, "There's something that's been on my heart for a while. I want to find a way for my company to partner with the church. We're already working with the city of Charlotte on efforts to help with affordable housing, but what if we started something to tie the church and the marketplace and the needs all together? How can we become the glue? People already come to the church all the time and ask for benevolence. But what about the ones who show up on Sunday and desperately need help but don't or won't ask for it? I feel like we could create some incredible synergy together."

Out of that conversation, in 2022, our realty company helped create a nonprofit ministry called Hope to Home. For so many churches, especially megachurches, it's quite easy for people to come in and out the doors but also remain invisible to the staff and most members. Campus pastors can easily get slammed with trying to connect with people and put out the fire of the day. Our goal for this ministry is for any families that come to the church who, for some reason, may be going through a tough time to find an advocate in us. A woman caught in domestic violence. A single mom behind on her rent. A family that doesn't have the money to pay the electricity bill in summer heat or for gas in the winter cold. In the development of this ministry, one of the most practical ways we discovered we could help people achieve their goals was to assist them in the American Dream of becoming first-time homeowners.

The rules of business and capitalism would say that no real estate firm would or should work closely with a church to help members get into a home. The rules would say that our real estate group could never bridge that gap and open those doors and that we shouldn't try. Yet, the relationships we built over the years through service and community leadership have allowed us to create this very opportunity.

Now, speaking to the cynical, some might say a real estate company would just use this as a stream for leads to increase sales and make a buck. But for us to keep the focus on always giving more than we take and on serving those in need in our area, the partnership covers all the bases for us to be able to take the right kind of action in our community—solving real problems for real people, just because God has given us the resources. Trust me, we don't need to create more business through smaller deals; this is a service to people, pure and simple.

Hope to Home was yet another vehicle for our business to serve the church and improve the lives of our neighbors throughout Charlotte.

Next, I want to cover a few added truths regarding gratitude.

From "What I Get" to "What I Give"

In our culture and in the marketplace, when we constantly work to give more than we take, the rules of the game won't matter. There are countless written and unwritten rules and codes of conduct that keep us bound up and "in our place." But when we can put the focus on giving, that is a game changer. In the case of creating Hope to Home, the bottom-line goal of helping people who are struggling overruled all the questions and discussions of "Could we? Should we? Can we?" because we just did!

There's an old saying that goes, "The world is changed by those who show up." Those who show up are there to help, not debate the rules. That's why, no matter on which side of the political aisle you stand today, you're likely frustrated. Most of us are tired of the rules and just want someone to give more than they take, to see some action, some kind of change, to show up and step up.

Another simple truth that connects to gratitude is that we will always have what we need when we help people get what they need. So often over the years, as I've talked with high-capacity agents about their goals, I've heard things like, "I want to sell a hundred homes this next year," "I want to make a hundred thousand dollars," "I want to retire by the time I'm fifty," and so on. Of course, goals are great, and we all need them to inspire and gauge our growth. But the real challenge always comes in making these a reality, for us to take those goals and change them from me-focused statements into others-focused questions.

"I want to sell a hundred homes this next year" becomes "I want to identify one hundred individuals or families whom I can serve by helping them with their housing needs this year."

"I want to make a hundred thousand dollars" becomes "I want to find one new inroad every month in our community where I can expand my network, from the inner city to the suburbs."

"I want to retire by the time I'm fifty" becomes "I want to make enough money to be able to spend the second half of my professional life volunteering and meeting needs in the community."

Semantics? Maybe. But I guarantee you that changing the perspective from "what I get" to "what I give" will make a difference in everything from motive to mission. Shifting the focus from "What do I need?" to "What do others need?" will make a major difference in the choices we make. When all our goal statements begin with an "I" mentality, we will naturally always look for what we can gain in most every deal. When we trade out "I" with "others," we can train ourselves to seek out opportunities to give, serve, change, and show up for the right reasons. I have found that when we take on that mindset, the money will follow, but it won't be the focus.

When everything is going great, when sales are coming in, deals are closing, and money is flowing, it's so easy to ride the wave and maintain the status quo. But nothing changes our focus quite like some adversity. A little trouble can ignite a fire where comfort has kept us captive. When we have to sacrifice, we also have to start asking ourselves some hard questions.

I want to close this principle by offering some practical suggestions and examples of things I have done that you can do as well.

Expressing and Displaying Gratitude in My Business

When most people in the marketplace make the sale and move on to the next customer, we continue past the transaction in these ways:

- Checking in monthly
- Following up and following through when we find out a client needs help
- Sending invitations to client appreciation events, fundraisers, community events, and other activities we are involved with
- Making introductions and connections to help with jobs, promotions, internships, universities, and other opportunities for advancement
- Offering financial advice when appropriate
- Occasionally, quietly helping someone financially when we become aware of a dire need

One of the strategies I have used for staying grateful for my clients is to remind myself and my team of how many other options they have with all the other agencies in the metro-Charlotte area. You can't ever start thinking you're so big or so good or that you're the best game in town because then you lose your edge and your gratitude. That attitude can send people to everyone else who's still hungry for business.

I attempt each day in the marketplace to focus on adding value outside of the transaction and even outside of real estate. I enjoy being the present friend who works to learn what people need in their marriage, for their kids, for their health, their wealth, faith, and any aspect of life I can.

My lack of relationships growing up still causes me to be so grateful for each relationship I have now. I hope that the person on the other side of the relationship feels that gratitude, whether members of my team, friends, or peers.

One of the ways we work to be examples of gratitude to our new agents and employees is to have our experienced agents and loan officers share their experiences, showing their own gratitude, to bring perspective to those who are new to the industry or to our team. This practice helps bring them into our culture. This means so much more coming from their peers than from me as the owner.

Whenever any of our agents voice frustrations because a client took a house off the market, decided not to make an offer, or made some other decision that affects us, I always remind the agent of the other side: be grateful that the client trusts us with one of their biggest financial decisions, one of the most important transactions of their lives. We need to stay grateful that the client chose and trusted us when there are over fifteen thousand other agents in the greater Charlotte region.

As the founder of the company, I try hard to lead by example, being present in the office, working alongside my team, offering assistance, and, as the saying goes, not being afraid to get my hands dirty.

All clients want the experience of having top-notch customer service during the transaction, and that can only happen when the deal is right. Yet we should also focus outside of the transaction, expressing gratitude in as many ways as possible for the relationship.

There are great companies all over the world that are known for five-star customer service that do not focus on the client outside the transaction. So, if you want your business to have a secret weapon, then go where the real relationship is built—when there is nothing to gain and no money is being made. Add value as the expert while being the friend who is always present and attentive to their needs.

Expressing and Displaying Gratitude at Home

Because of how much Jessica and I had been blessed, by the time we had children, both our sons were born with far more than we could ever have imagined possible when we were kids. For that reason, we are constantly working so hard to instill humility and gratitude in them. We are both well aware that it can't be "taught as much as caught."

Even at their young age, we take our boys with us to any church, ministry, and service projects. We want to show them firsthand the adversity that so many face, to give them a real-world perspective of gratitude for what they have been given.

One of the practical things we have done is to give out blessing bags—a sort of care package for an individual or a family in need. Depending on the situation, we include a small amount of money, a toothbrush and toothpaste, snacks, and other items, trying to meet practical needs through a small gift. One day, while handing out some from our car with the boys in the back seat, we encountered a family with kids around the ages of ours. Jessica literally took the kid's toys that were in the car and the shoes off their feet to give the family, along with some money and gift cards. She told the boys we had plenty more toys and shoes back home, but these people needed them now, and we weren't sure we would see them again.

We have an ongoing question in our home that we frequently ask, "Are you being humble or proud?" We want to communicate to our sons the characteristics of Jesus, to which Jessica and I strive to be obedient.

Besides the stories in the Gospels that we read to the boys, we also talk regularly about how Christ was born with very little, how he grew up and walked among people from criminals to the helpless, from the rich to the poor and everyone in between. Jesus didn't show favorites even though he did have friends, just like we do. Jesus was willing to die on the cross so that we could be forgiven for our sins even though he did not deserve the punishment he took on. We, just like the disciples, don't deserve his grace and mercy.

No matter what your goals and no matter where you are today, if you focus on what you are grateful for in your life and what you can give out of that life, you'll find purpose, passion, and a fresh perspective for life and work.

In closing, the apostle Paul constantly expressed gratitude for what Christ had saved him *from* and saved him *to*. I am continually challenged by his attitude toward life.

> I thank Christ Jesus our Lord, who has given me strength to do his work. He considered me trustworthy and appointed me to serve him, even though I used to blaspheme the name of Christ. In my insolence, I persecuted his people. But God had mercy on me because I did it in ignorance and unbelief. Oh, how generous and gracious our Lord was!

> He filled me with the faith and love that come from Christ Jesus.
>
> This is a trustworthy saying, and everyone should accept it: "Christ Jesus came into the world to save sinners"—and I am the worst of them all. But God had mercy on me so that Christ Jesus could use me as a prime example of his great patience with even the worst sinners. Then others will realize that they, too, can believe in him and receive eternal life. All honor and glory to God forever and ever! He is the eternal King, the unseen one who never dies; he alone is God. Amen. (1 Timothy 1:12–17)

APPLICATION EXERCISE

Let's make this exercise as simple as possible.

Go back through the examples I've offered and either decide which ones you could introduce and adopt in your own business or use mine as inspiration to create your own. Write down your commitments and ideas.

Refer to my personal examples for our family in expressing gratitude and either decide which ones you could introduce and adopt in your own family (or personal life if you're single) or use ours as inspiration to create your own. Write down your commitments and ideas.

12

PRINCIPLE #6
BE A FRIEND BEFORE BEING THE EXPERT

A longtime, dear friend, who has been very successful in the marketplace for many years, once said to me, "David, I want you to know that you're one of my *five* friends."

Puzzled, I asked, "Well, you must know thousands of people. How can I possibly be one of *only* five?"

He answered, "It's true that I *know* a lot of people, good people, out there, but there are five among those whom I count as true friends. With you being one."

While I was grateful he considered me to be such a close friend, I really didn't understand how that could be true for this man who is loved and respected by so many. Yet now that my own network has grown exponentially in the marketplace, I get it—more than ever. When any of us look at what it means to have a *real* friend, one who we know genuinely cares about us and carries no agenda, that narrows the number significantly. As we honestly consider these standards, the numbers dwindle quickly. In your own circles, how many people would you consider to be actual friends?

While it doesn't necessarily reflect friendship, this concept reminds me of the story of Gideon's army in the book of Judges. God sifted the men gathered with the unlikely warrior, reducing the number of troops until Gideon was down to the real core of the ones whom God and Gideon could count on. He started with thirty-two thousand men. At the first cull, he lost twenty-two thousand and was left with ten thousand. Down at the water's edge, the final cut dropped ninety-seven hundred more. Just three hundred remained.

Little did Gideon know that while standing confidently among the tens of thousands, he really only had three hundred whom he could count on. Put to the test, the truth was revealed. And Gideon won the battle to which God called him with the faithful few, those men whom God had chosen, not Gideon (see Judges 7).

To apply this Bible story to today's culture, Oxford University psychology professor Robin Dunbar studied 3,375 Facebook users in the UK between the ages of eighteen and sixty-five. Each person in the sample group had an average of 150 "friends." Digging into their lives, culling and cutting, if you will, the researchers found that 13.6 of those "friends" would express sympathy during an emotional crisis, and the Facebook users considered only 4.1 to be dependable in a real-life circumstance.

Dunbar wrote, "Respondents who had unusually large networks did not increase the numbers of close friendships they had, but rather added more loosely defined acquaintances into their friendship circle." The article reporting the study goes on to say, "Younger users are likely to have more Facebook friends, but older users tend to have more friends in real life. That is because social media encourages 'promiscuous friending' of individuals who often have very tenuous links."[7]

Applying the math, Dunbar's percentages aren't far from Gideon's.

The takeaway here is not to judge the crowd that has *gathered around you* but to get honest about who is actually *standing with you.* Love them all, but get real about who truly loves you as a friend. That way, you won't get blindsided in your next battle when you need backup that you can count on to show up, stand up, and step up. In a crisis, don't get angry with those who walk away, but be grateful for those who stay. Just as my friend told me, have five among the thousands.

Especially in our market-driven culture, most professionals today count many of their business acquaintances as friends. But is that a real friend? The same concept can be true for those whom people call their pastors. You can ask someone who his or her pastor is, and the person will give the name of the one who holds the title at the church. But then if you ask the same person, "If you were suddenly in a crisis at three o'clock in the morning, whom would you call?" that answer is much more likely to name the person's *actual* pastor.

Now, let's switch from evaluating friends to examining experts. We live in a day in which more people than ever are claiming to be "experts" in so many areas, to the point where we have never been more distrusting of the actual experts! We should all strive to hit our ten thousand hours—or any standard of credibility that marks our particular industry—that mark us as authorities with expertise. But the extra mile, the choice that adds value, is in being a friend first and the expert second.

The old saying "No one likes a know-it-all" is so true, but there's a distinct line between know-it-alls and experts. Jesus was an expert on literally everything, yet he told his disciples, "I no longer call you servants...Instead, I have called you friends" (John 15:15 NIV). And what did that ragtag group of folks go on to do? Change the known world. Like I said earlier, the disciples had to overcome the familiarity of Jesus being their friend in order to see that he was the Son of God. But once that perspective took hold, Jesus allowed them yet another perspective. By the time of his ascension, their obedience wasn't to the expert they followed but to their friend, out of deep, endearing loyalty.

The Power of Three

For this principle, I want to go back to my original three standards that I adopted on my drive from DC to Charlotte:

1. Be the friend.
2. Be the expert.
3. Be present.

Let's review and expand on these concepts.

In starting out with being the friend first, a major mistake I see so many people make is saying, "Oh, I'm everyone's friend. I try to be nice to everybody." I liken that sentiment to a beauty contestant saying she wants world peace. Sounds nice, great answer, but what are you really going to *do* to offer some solutions for world peace to happen? When you say you are "everyone's friend," my question is "How many calls do you get in an average month from someone asking for personal advice?" We can't confuse being a friend with simply being extroverted. I say extroverted even though a lot of salespeople who are actually introverts in their personality act extroverted to make a sale. Being outgoing or extroverted is required for most professionals, yet if you tend to call yourself "everyone's friend," be honest with yourself about whom you are actually friends with.

Then there's the mindset of keeping business and personal separate. Many people believe that friends don't want to work with friends. At least from my experience, nothing could be further from the truth. If someone wants to keep any business from you because you're friends, what that person might actually be communicating is that he or she either does not trust that you're the expert or doesn't feel like you would have enough time to help. Friends may have the impression that you're not present professionally if you constantly have too much going on, are scattered, or always show up late. Even if they know you care, they don't know how much. So, to that person, you aren't the expert. That drives their decision to separate business and personal.

When any of us meet someone for the first time, we have to make a choice to begin to build the relationship or not. To become the friend, we have to earn the opportunity. Being the expert, you have to add enough value that the person drops his or her guard and starts letting you in so you can create the connection. As a real estate agent, I can meet someone at an open house or someone who is referred to me by another client. Maybe I meet the person at church or some community event and he or she asks for my advice about real estate. From the very first conversation, I can start to add value as the expert. Friendship can then come out of that experience.

I have found that of the three—friend, expert, and being present—most people will focus on *one* of the three. I want to ask you to honestly evaluate yourself as we look at what it means to focus on only one, meaning the other two are diminished or absent.

"I'm a Friend."
(But Not an Expert and Not Present)

An example of being only the friend would be the person who knows everybody in the community and whom everyone "loves." So he becomes a salesperson at a local car dealership, believing he will dominate in sales. Finding out where he is and what he is doing, people start to drop by or call, but he can't answer questions about the vehicles because he's done zero due diligence to learn the products. Then as a busy, type-A mover and shaker, he doesn't return phone calls or respond to emails. He's never present. The outcome? In three months tops, he's moved on from selling cars. Being the guy everyone knows and loves is the catalyst to get people in the door, but the majority of the time, it won't close the deal.

Think about it—how many friends do you have whom you wouldn't consider doing business with? Consider *why* you wouldn't contact that person. Now, take that info and turn it on yourself. Who wouldn't call *you* for what you do, and why? You know you're a friend, so *how* are you not the expert? How are you not present? Keep in mind that this principle is not about evaluating others but about getting honest about others' perception of you and what you can do about changing that.

Here's a real-world example of all three connecting when the "friend" was already in place and the opportunity came to connect the other two. In a midsize city in Indiana, a local law enforcement officer had put in twenty-five years and decided he was ready to retire from that line of work. A local car dealership owner called and asked him if he was going to actually stop working or if he might be open to a new career. The ex-officer said he was still fairly young, was healthy, and could use the money, so a new challenge would be great. The owner responded to his answer, "Then why don't you come sell cars for me?"

The ex-officer answered, "But I don't know anything about selling *anything*!"

The owner reassured him, "You know everyone in the county and have a reputation of integrity and honesty. I can't create that in someone, but I can teach a guy how to sell cars!"

Before long, the *friend* who lived a life of being *present* in the community became the *expert* at selling cars. As a result, he discovered a second successful career that was far less dangerous.

"I'm an Expert." (But Not a Friend and Not Present)

A classic example of being only the expert is the renowned surgeon who thrives on being a successful and revered expert in his or her field but who has a horrendous bedside manner. Five stars on ability. One star on care. Human suffering is just a means to establishing job security. Emotional distance and lack of presence are very common traits in professionals who ascribe to this dynamic. The focus is on knowledge and building a name, not on the patients and their needs.

The 1991 film *Regarding Henry*, starring Harrison Ford and Annette Benning, written by J. J. Abrams, is about a narcissistic, powerful, wealthy attorney who has lost all regard for people, including his own wife and daughter. He had just recently won a malpractice suit, representing a hospital that destroyed the lives of the victim's family. When the attorney (Ford's character) gets shot in the head during a store robbery gone wrong, he survives but has brain damage, creating a childlike state. Over time as he begins to recover, he finds out who he once was—the expert with no friends who was never present for anyone. While his life appeared to be ruined, it was actually saved.

So many people get caught up in being successful in their careers, slowly losing regard for others as they become obsessed with status, wealth, and power. Particularly in our Western culture, this has become an epidemic in so many areas of the marketplace. We have to constantly be reminded that being an expert in what we do does not mean we have to be arrogant or selfish. In fact, being an expert can put us in an even better position to serve people. The more we know, the more we can help.

Being the expert in a transaction and offering great customer service is awesome. Yet outside the deal, if there is no real connection, what reason is there for a client to continue the relationship? Someone with a better deal or better sales pitch or more compelling product can come along and easily replace us. In your own life, there are likely people that you can always call anytime you need Product A. Why is that? But then anytime you need Product B, you don't return to the same vendor but start from scratch, looking for where to buy it. Why is that? These are important human dynamics to learn from when making our own choices, and they can help us improve our approach as well as others' perception of us.

The true "value add" is when you are the friend *before* the transaction, the expert *in* the transaction, and, once again, the friend *after* the transaction. That also provides ample proof that you are always present in the relationship. A friendship maintained. An expert available.

Presence throughout. You are not just good at one of the three but *all* three. That's the secret sauce on the Big Mac.

This triple threat is even vital in our own families. With my wife Jessica, I want to be her best friend, but I also need to be the expert husband. The only way to stay her best friend and keep being the expert in her life is to stay present as well. I need to *keep* knowing as much as I *can* know about her. The communication style that she responds to best and how she communicates to me. Her love language. How she needs some time to herself each day and how I can make sure she has that. Those things require my presence—physically, mentally, emotionally, and spiritually.

When I'm with her, I have to pay attention to what she is saying, what she is *not* saying, what her eyes and her body language are telling me, including how she stands and her visual cues, positive and negative. I can't just communicate my way. I have to communicate her way. More than anywhere else in our lives, with our families, we need to be the friend, be the expert, and be present.

None of us is going to be able to be strong in all three, so confession time for me: in my own life, my biggest struggle is the third piece—being present.

Small Town, Big Lesson

One of my greatest challenges on this subject came in 2014. Our family moved further south, deeper into the suburbs, away from metro Charlotte. Feeling more of a sense of community in our new area, I told Jessica that I wanted to serve on a broader scale. After exploring all my options, I decided to run for mayor of Marvin, North Carolina.

After filing the paperwork, announcing my candidacy, and putting in many hours of due diligence, I went into campaign mode, firing on all cylinders. I knocked on what felt like *every* resident's door. By election day, the folks helping me estimated the number to be around four thousand homes. I spoke at receptions in neighborhoods all around the area. I was allowed access to so many people from my years of building relationships as an agent. As is the norm in politics, I had to raise campaign funds. Once again, from my connections and having raised so much money for charities over the years, I was able to bring in more campaign contributions than anyone ever had in the county. Because the numbers were made public, my run began to get attention across the state.

During my campaign, I spoke with a friend who knows the ins and outs of politics. When I shared the story and the numbers I had raised, he responded, "I wish you would've told me sooner how small the town was and how many people are there. You should have run for a bigger office. That amount of money makes more sense if you're running for governor!" Hearing his counsel, I stopped taking contributions. After every speech or campaign stop, I literally started saying, "Please don't give me your money," which is a very strange thing for people to hear a wannabe politician say.

I'm going to go ahead and cut to the chase here—even with all this valiant effort, I lost the race for mayor of Marvin, North Carolina.

How? With all that exposure, support, and money raised?

Because I was new to the community and had no history yet, I was introduced to people as an expert. That was the only filter available through which they could see me. For the average person in that small community, I was no one's friend. They didn't know *me*. And they were just learning *about* me through one filter. I mistakenly thought that my reputation as a business owner in Charlotte would also somehow help them know my heart as their friend. But so many of them couldn't understand why I'd work so hard to get a job that paid so little. There had to be a catch. I couldn't blame them for making that assumption. That's why the majority of the residents voted for the local guy they had known for years, not the new outsider from the city they didn't know at all. Makes total sense, right?

But here's where the real learning curve came in.

Toward the end of the campaign, one friend called me to say, "Hey, man, we're getting ready to buy a new house. When we close, we want to have y'all over. We can celebrate you becoming mayor."

All I heard was that he didn't call me to buy his house. I said, "Wait…what? Is someone else on my team helping you? I didn't know about this."

His response was "Oh, we knew you wouldn't have time for us with the campaign and all."

His perception of my life was that I was too busy with other endeavors to be present as a real estate agent. He didn't question my friendship or my ability as a real estate agent, just my presence.

I also found out later that while I was campaigning, another friend had sold his house after finding another agent online. When I asked him why he didn't contact me, he answered, "You were running for mayor. I assumed you'd win and be done with real estate." I was shocked. But perception *is* reality.

Someone else called me and asked, "My granddaughter is buying her first home—a condo. I just have a quick question for you about the HOA fee. Is two hundred a month too much?"

Once again, my response was "Wait, your granddaughter is buying a condo? Why didn't you call me?"

He answered, "Oh, it's at a small price point. Too small a deal for you to bother with now."

No matter how much I tried to assure him that his *perception* was wrong, the *assumption* had already been made, and I lost the deal. Why? Not being a friend? No. Not being the expert? No, he called me because he knew I would know the answer. The problem was my lack of presence.

On the morning after election night, I got a text from a guy in a nearby town that read, "Hey, David, I'm sure you're discouraged that you lost last night, but let me give you some good news. Our $2 million home is your listing if you want it. We couldn't give it to the mayor of a neighboring town, but we can give it to the real estate expert we trust."

As the mayoral candidate in my new community, I might have been the expert, but I was not the friend. During that season, focusing solely on the campaign, I was not present in my business. My unintentional focus on just one of the three in both places caused me to lose in so many areas. In the end, I'm still glad I tried my hand at politics because God doesn't waste anything we give him. But I learned another valuable lesson on the power of presence and maintaining the balance of all three.

Installing Safeguards

Whichever of these three we may find to be our weakness, our blind spot, we have to find ways to strengthen and support that area. In this next section, I'll share some of the ways I have built in safeguards for me to be present. One of the biggest enemies we face when trying to accomplish any or all three of these is time. Our culture is so fast-paced and double-booked that the biggest detriment to being a friend, being an expert, and especially being present is battling our schedules.

When it comes to money, the amounts we make are going to widely vary. You might be reading this book to find a little hope as a budding entrepreneur who is struggling to pay rent right now. Or you might be a multimillionaire looking for a few new nuggets of inspiration. The factors that would distinguish us from one another are many. But the one area we all have in common is time. We are given seven days in each week with 24 hours in each day. That is 168 hours every week. That's what we each have to work with, no matter how many other resources we have or don't have.

Let's say you go to your local big-box home improvement store and find the aisle where they sell chains. Whether you choose the metal or plastic variety, think about rolling out 168 links on the concrete floor and cutting the chain off after the final link. If each link is two inches long, the total chain would be twenty-eight feet—almost the height of a three-story building.

Stretched out in a line to represent the hours in your week, think about how you divide up your time on any given day in any given week by using the links to represent your choices. When we look at time linearly, with each link of the chain being an hour, it can change the perspective of how we view our choices. After you remove the links for sleeping, eating, and other basic things you do to maintain your life, how many links are committed to becoming a friend? To being an expert? And, if you're like me, the biggest challenge is how many links in a week I am being truly present, whether as a friend, an expert, or both.

Demand for our time affects us all too. One day I got a text from a good friend, who has also been a client over the years, that said, "So I have to go through your assistant now? You're one of my best friends."

I found out that while my assistant was, of course, working to protect my schedule, she had noticed that I was going to be needed in the office at the time he and I were scheduled to get coffee. She had reached out to him to move the meeting. I know for a lot of business owners, that might be an acceptable method of communication, but for me, it violates my principles. Because my friend communicated directly with me, I was able to resolve the issue.

That's just another example of how we can begin to place a layer of "protection" around us and start to only be available as the expert. Putting up those personal firewalls, so to speak, usually just ends up doing harm to relationships. When I, along with my staff, begin to vet people based solely on current "importance," I've never seen that become a positive move in the right direction. Protection? Sure. Prevention? No. There's a difference.

Another way we can begin to lose connection and presence is when we stop saying yes to spending time with people who want to talk business in a recreational or personal setting. Some examples are when someone wants to take Jessica and me out for dinner or asks me to go play golf on a Saturday morning. Of course, we have to decide when those are right for us and our families, but we should never get to the place where we *always* say no because soon people will stop asking. And when they stop asking, you quickly become out of sight, out of mind. Because of my family commitments and busy life, these are some examples of where I can struggle the most to say yes, to agree to presence. The key is always seeking balance in *all* things.

My primary mode for staying present is to focus all my time and attention on the people who are already in my life: friends, clients, and people who have reached out to me for one reason or another. Through proactive communication, I work to check in with them regularly, as I have talked about previously. I work to meet them where they are and make it about them. I try to listen intently and be ready to be the expert when they need me to be. But I work to be a friend and be present at least every thirty days through communication.

As I stay committed to connection, I have found that new relationships will always be born out of my current relationships, as people offer, "Let me connect you to him," "I referred her to you," or "You two really should know one another." It's the quintessential stone dropped in the water—the ripples will naturally flow out from the initial impact.

Another safeguard I have placed in my life is, if at all possible, to leave a fifteen-minute buffer before I go into my next meeting or call so I can adjust my thoughts and shift the energy. If you go straight out of an intense situation into a setting where you are meeting someone new or out of a laid-back hang into a negotiation, your demeanor could be affected. A major part of being present is not carrying anything into a meeting that could distract you or affect how you should focus and deal with your current interaction. If you tend to allow your emotions to strongly affect your mood, this one piece of advice could be worth the price of this book.

For example, if you have a twelve o'clock lunch, plan to get there at 11:45. What if you hit every red light? What if you walk in right at noon and have to go to the bathroom? We all know how it feels to be waiting on someone who comes in the door like their hair is on fire. That's a clear indication that the person's thoughts are somewhere else—where they just came from or where they're going after you. Not a good look to start a productive time together. Being present means being prepared and ready.

Another safeguard I have is trying to respond before my next meal to anyone who has reached out to me. If I get an email at 9:30 a.m. and I have a lunch meeting at 11:30, I need to respond to the person before I eat lunch. *Why?* This accomplishes two things: I leave no one waiting on me, and I can enjoy my meal without being distracted by the people I've missed or to whom I still owe a response. There are always going to be impatient and unreasonable people whom you can't please, but I've found this to be a really helpful way for me to stay present *and* current.

Lastly, if I put something on my calendar, I don't take it off—outside of some emergency, of course. When we start making it a practice to move people around according to what we feel is most important at the moment, that leads to a lack of presence. The juggling can also create a level of ongoing chaos. If someone else has to cancel or reschedule, we can't control that. But let it be the other person. We don't want to get a reputation of being someone people can't count on to follow through with a meeting because they think, *Well, we'll see if he shows. He always reschedules at the last minute.* Bottom line—if the person was important enough for you to put on your calendar two weeks ago, what should change that today?

Here's the summary: If you already know someone, be the friend first. But if you don't know the person, then lead as the expert who gives more than you take. Friendships can come from being the expert. Trust, credibility, and respect are all great building blocks for a strong relationship. And to again drive home the point—the secret sauce is being present.

I completely understand that in today's lightning-fast, blink-and-you-miss-it world, what I have shared in this principle is a tall order for many of us. But the bottom line is that it can be done, and life can become better because of the effort. You can be the exception in the culture and be exceptional in all your circles of influence by doing so.

Let's close this principle with some simple truths:

- Don't make it about work even when it's about work.
- Be yourself; don't sell yourself.
- Meet people where they are and assume nothing about them before you get to know them.
- If God places someone in your life who has a need, reach out to everyone else whom he has placed in your life to help with that need.
- Don't let thirty days go by without reaching out to those whom God has placed in your life.
- When a conflict arises with someone, learn how to overcome the circumstances rather than place blame.

APPLICATION EXERCISE

What is your *strongest* position—being a friend, being the expert, or being present? Explain.

What is your *weakest* position—being a friend, being the expert, or being present? Explain.

What is one practical piece of advice I shared that you could implement to be more present?

In what ways could being more present help your business?

In what ways could being more present help your family or personal life?

13

PRINCIPLE #7
IT'S NOT ABOUT THE DEAL BUT ABOUT DOING THE RIGHT THING

One of the jokes we often make today among friends is to say, "Man, you should have your own reality show." Well, in 2013, I was offered the opportunity to become the "star" or the focal character or whatever they call the lead in those. The working title was *Welcome to Charlotte.* The concept was to produce "a day in the life" episodes of a successful real estate agent, featuring our beautiful city. Initially when I heard the concept, I saw no red flags or issues and, of course, knew it could be great for marketing. So I agreed to shoot the pilot and went along with the producer to see what might happen. Honestly, at the onset, I couldn't see a good reason to say no.

After the pilot was shopped to networks, two major cable networks expressed interest in the show. The producer called me and said, "All right, David, we're gonna get picked up by a network. We'll shoot how you help everyone from first-time buyers to high-profile clients. We'll show you selling everything from mansions to starter homes. You're going to be able to talk about your service projects and fundraisers, and we'll also want to include your family." Everything he mentioned was just a summary of my actual life, so that all sounded great. But then here's where things got a bit dicey.

If you watch much reality TV, you won't be surprised at what came next. The producer said, "We just did one season on VH1 with a national sports hero, and honestly, it turned out to be very boring. He's a great guy like you, but there was no real drama. So, for that reason, his show is not getting picked up for a second season, which is where we actually start making money. So, David, we're going to need to insert some drama, some conflict, for your show to succeed."

Concerned, I asked, "What exactly do you mean by *drama*?"

He continued, "Well, like there's a lot of ladies in your realty group. We could shoot you going out to have some drinks with some of them after work, having some fun with them…without your wife. That kind of thing. If you're smart, David, you'll agree to do this. It could be huge for you."

He could tell I was hesitant, so he asked me to think about it over the next week. I did, and, of course, I prayed about it too. Jessica and I processed through the opportunity at length. Quickly, I knew I had to call him to say, "I prayed about this, and I don't need a week to make a decision. I can't do it. I'm sorry, but the answer is no. I'm going to pass."

His frustrated response was "Well, I think you're going to regret this."

The producer moved on to another state, found a cast of locals, changed the name, and, bottom line, created a hit TV show with millions of viewers each week. In that world, the guy certainly knew what he was doing.

After seeing the success of the show and being genuinely happy for him, I called and offered, "Hey, congratulations. Looks like you got exactly what you wanted."

To which he responded, "Now, don't you feel bad about missing such a great opportunity? I warned you."

I smiled and answered, "No, I don't. I really don't. Glad everything turned out right for us both."

Here's the moral to that story for me: The show could have created an incredible income stream, launched an amazing national marketing campaign for free, and made me into a household name, as they say. Yet, no matter how lucrative the deal was, it was not at all the right thing for me, my family, or our businesses.

That's not to say that all reality TV shows can't work for Christ followers. Not at all. The Robertson family used their *Duck Dynasty* fame to get the gospel out to so many people all over the world and be incredibly entertaining too. Today, even with the show no longer in production, their platform remains a massive megaphone for Christ. The deal was right for the Robertsons but not right for the Hoffmans.

I shared my close call with reality show fame as a big-picture example of when the right thing is to say no even when countless others would line up to say yes, regardless of how big an opportunity might appear. Now, I want to talk about how this truth plays out in all the businesses I own or co-own, day in and day out.

From day one, while our goal is to close deals, we won't sacrifice doing the right thing. To be clear, the right thing is determined by whether the circumstances line up with God and his Word, not what the culture deems to be right or correct. The truth according to society has become such a moving target that it is no longer something we can base our lives upon. For so many issues, what was true and best twenty years ago, society now considers wrong, and what society considered to be right is now wrong. I personally prefer to have a standard for truth that never changes. As Hebrews 13:8 states, "Jesus Christ is the same yesterday, today, and forever." And, once again, we find wisdom in the words of Solomon:

> My child, listen to me and do as I say,
> and you will have a long, good life.
> I will teach you wisdom's ways
> and lead you in straight paths.
> When you walk, you won't be held back;
> when you run, you won't stumble.
> Take hold of my instructions; don't let them go.
> Guard them, for they are the key to life.
> (Proverbs 4:10–13)

What tends to drive most of the deals we make every day in our marketplace? The answer, of course, is money—making a buck and turning a profit—because we all have to make a living. We do what we do to make sure we can take care of our families, pay our bills, and live our lives. There's nothing wrong with that. The problems arise when selfishness, greed, and corruption enter the picture. We've all heard the sayings, whether tongue-in-cheek or true, like, "He'll do whatever it takes to close a deal" and "She'd sell out her own grandmother to make a sale." All too often, money and the battle for a winning position determine the parameters of a transaction. From sales contracts to lawsuits, the deal points drive the outcome, as in who can win, who can gain, and who can get or give the best deal.

I have found that when simply doing the right thing is the catalyst, that is a game changer. In our current climate, some interpret the right thing to mean that you win or at least get the upper hand. But I'm talking about a countercultural approach of making sure the right thing is what's best for the *other* person or party. The right thing is about the relationship.

The Lord has given me a unique sense of empathy or mercy, a gift to be able to meet people where they are. While I work hard to be the same guy everywhere, I also want to adapt to the people I meet. For example, when my Jewish friends found out I had become a Christ follower, at first, they were critical. But, after a while, they saw my commitment was real and that a transformation was taking place in my life. They realized it wasn't an impulse decision, a fad, or some whim. One person told me, "Wow, you actually seem to have a relationship." My background has allowed me to draw several Jewish people into our real estate company, which I love. That worldview drives me to love my neighbor in all things, including transactions.

For the remainder of this principle, and as we begin to wrap up the book, I want to share five relatable and practical truths that I hope you can apply in your own circles.

1. The right thing will always be the best decision to make.
2. The right thing is finding the win for the other person, not for you.
3. The right thing is anticipating what someone needs without waiting on them to ask.
4. The right thing may go against your idols.

5. The right thing is to always focus on the good in a person, no matter how badly circumstances may go.

1. The Best Decision

I get it. That seems *too* obvious, right? But let me explain by offering some examples of what we all know can become the rationalizations we argue inside our own minds.

The right thing to do is *this*, but if I do *that*, I can make more money.

The right thing to do is *this*, but if I do *that*, I can get another step up the corporate ladder.

The right thing to do is *this*, but if I do *that*, I can beat my competitor.

The right thing is to stay at home with my family for my son's birthday, but if I go to the convention in Vegas that weekend, I can make more connections.

The right thing is to head home and have dinner with my spouse, but if I go out for drinks with that group, maybe I can show them why I'm the best person for the promotion.

In my experience, when we really do know what the right thing is but we have this other option, have something else on the table, or are just lingering as a distraction, the vast majority of the time, we need to go with what we *know* to be the right thing, the best decision, and not take the risk with a plan B.

I also understand that "the right thing" has never been more subjective than in our current culture. But that's exactly why I'm allowing for each of us to know within our heart of hearts what the truth *actually* is versus whatever we might rationalize when we are tempted to do something different. If I or any other author, speaker, or business professional has to begin teaching ethics and morals, we're all in trouble anyway.

Working with a large team of agents, I'm often asked to help problem solve various issues. A common scenario goes something like this: an agent comes to me and says that his clients want to go under contract to sell their house right away, but they also want to make as much money as possible. Of course, here's the issue: that's what all sellers want, to get a contract ASAP for the maximum amount of money.

So all I do is ask questions: "Okay, what's more important to the clients? Getting a certain price or securing the contract?"

The agent may say, "Well, they signed a contingency on a new house, and the deadline is next Monday."

My response: "Sounds like it's more important to get a contract this week, which means they may need to take less money. Ask them what their bottom line is so you know what they'll approve."

My job is to cut through the emotions, the noise, and the options by simply asking the right questions that can help my agent arrive at the real priority. I'd rather ask questions of my team to help them arrive at their own answers.

Quite often, the best decision won't be what a lot of people think it should be. Several times throughout these pages, I have mentioned working with pro athletes and other high-profile clients, but I have also turned down some opportunities other people would have loved to take. There have been times when I knew by the person's reputation that the transaction would not be a good experience for *my* team. If I know someone is going to be rude, disrespectful, and entitled, I have no problem avoiding taking him or her on as a client. If most agents got a call that a famous pro athlete wanted to list or buy a $4 million home, the obvious "right thing" would be to jump on the opportunity. But it will not always be what you think it will be.

Over the years, we have had several opportunities to work with local and national builders to be the agency for an entire community or neighborhood. But whether the issue became having to offer a different fee structure that might cause us to be unfair to our other clients or some other potential integrity dilemma, we have given up the account, forfeiting media attention, guaranteed commissions, and job security for years. What may appear to be such a right thing at the onset can turn into a major wrong thing.

When I sent one owner an email detailing that we were parting ways and why, he quickly responded, "Hey, I think you accidentally sent me this and it was supposed to go to someone else. I assume this was not for me." He couldn't imagine anyone would pull out of such a lucrative deal. Now, if you're keeping score, I have been called crazy a number of times for my decisions. But that's exactly why I'm sharing all these principles with you. I don't live by *accident* but by *intention*. I live by relationships, not rules. Especially the marketplace rules of the game.

As a Christ follower, sometimes you have to leave a difficult relationship because you realize it's not one that God wants in your life. In some instances, he will use it to teach you what *not* to be. Unfortunately, there are times when we have to recognize a toxic relationship and take the necessary action. Needless to say, there is an incredible responsibility to end such a relationship without harming your witness or integrity.

The apostle Paul touched on this as well when he taught: "Do not repay anyone evil for evil. Be careful to do what is right in the eyes of everyone. If it is possible, as far as it depends on you, live at peace with everyone" (Romans 12:17–18 NIV).

Note his qualifiers—"if it is possible" and "as far as it depends on you." We cannot control what others will do or what their response might be. We are only called to do all we can to "live at peace."

2. Find the Win for Them

We often hear people talk about finding the win-win. This goes beyond that idea. The right thing is often not a win for *both* sides. Even if I don't get the deal and my clients decide it's better to stay in their house for the time being, that's the win for now. If my clients win, then I win too. If the right thing happens for them, that *is* the best decision.

For me, my faith in Christ has allowed me to know that when I look out for the other person, then God will take care of me no matter what. The deal is never my source; God is. That knowledge gives me the freedom to hold on to things very loosely.

That said, even if you don't share my belief system, which is totally fine, I can promise you that when people see you are out for them to win, your life and your business are going to improve over the long haul. Even the concept of karma in Eastern religions is based on the idea that whatever you do is going to create some sort of return.

Another major factor in being able to choose the win for the other person, regardless of how it may affect me, is how hard I have worked to remove fear from my life. My childhood and growing up conditioned me in such a way that when I got older, I had to realize there was no longer any need to fear. After *my* childhood, what should I be afraid of as an adult? First John 4:18–19 states, "Such love has no fear, because perfect love expels all fear. If we are afraid, it is for fear of punishment, and this shows that we have not fully experienced his perfect love. We love each other because he loved us first."

But once again, regardless of our belief system, fear can drive so many of our decisions. *Too* many of our decisions. Think about it—for all the statements I gave earlier, you could change the wording to "The right thing to do is this, but I'm *afraid* if I don't do that, then I won't have enough money or won't get the promotion or won't close the deal." *Do you see it?* We can insert "I'm afraid if I do or if I don't" into so many of our temptations to make the wrong move or even to potentially do the wrong thing for someone else. When we work to recognize and remove fear in our lives, we can make better decisions and, quite honestly, become better people. And better people do better business.

I want to be clear that I am not talking about the healthy fear we should have in our lives. We can better define healthy fear as a respect for the consequences of a circumstance. That's a God-given and positive emotion. I'm talking about unhealthy fear, which is the majority of what we all deal with. Fear of loss. Fear of being hurt. Fear of rejection. Negative and toxic emotions catalyze all those fears. Separating healthy fear (respect and recognition of a situation for protection) from the fears that can paralyze and penalize us is vital.

The marketplace is accustomed to the person with the highest price always being the winner in a bidding war. Five offers come in on a house, and unless the highest one has shaky financing or some other risk factor, the money will win. But when the right thing is the focus, far bigger and more important dynamics are at play.

Today, it has become customary for prospective buyers to shoot and send videos to sellers to communicate any emotional or social message they want the seller to know. A family can introduce themselves one by one and then say something like, "We love your home." The kids can say, "We hope that we can get to play in your backyard for years to come." The wife can say, "I see us celebrating the holidays, gathered around the table, looking at the Christmas tree under your beautiful high ceilings with the natural light. Because everything you've done with the home is gorgeous." I have seen heartfelt, authentically shared videos win out over higher bids on a number of occasions. The largest I have personally seen is when a seller chose a buyer with an emotional video over a buyer who offered $300,000 more. For some sellers, it just isn't about money but about peace of mind when transferring a home they love and have invested in to someone they feel good about. Relationships over rules.

For some people, tugging at their heartstrings works. For others, they receive peace of mind from more money down or a higher escrow, waiving a large list of repairs, or even allowing the sellers to rent the home back after closing so they have more time to move. A win often comes from the agents getting creative to meet needs.

Here's another "non-win-win" I've experienced. Some of my favorite clients have never hired me as a real estate agent. *What?* Yes, because when I met them, they were already in a home and happy there. But, as our connection grew, they began to refer me to other people. They speak highly about my business and my character but have never used my services because they don't need them yet. Seeing me spending a lot of time and energy, even possibly money, on someone who's never been a client might seem strange to some. But I may have sold five properties because of one relationship.

Over the years, after understanding someone's finances and goals, I've told many buyers that it's not the best time for them to buy a home. To focus on paying off debt, improving their credit scores, and making a more substantial down payment was the best thing—the right thing—for their family. Now, I can't do anything about whether they tell me they want the house. But I have to do the right thing for their sake, based on the knowledge I have at the time. On the other side of the market, I've also told people that I didn't think it was the best time to sell.

3. Anticipating Needs

There have been many times when I listened to my clients as they talked about their lives, their goals, and what was important to them. Here's one example of when I felt like I saw the need and offered before the ask.

"Hey, I understand you guys are looking for the right house here, but I want to at least offer you another option. Because you're moving to Charlotte from across the country and you don't yet know the city and all the different areas, I found a great deal on a short-term lease for an apartment in a nice area of town. It's fully furnished, so there's no rush in getting your stuff here. There would be no maintenance. This would significantly lower your stress in the move and give you some breathing room to get to know the city. You could start to find some relationships and a church. I'd be happy to introduce you to some people. Maybe don't worry about the sale right now? Just come here and get acclimated. Then you'll be able to make a better decision in a few months about where you want to live. If you want to move forward on a house, great, but I wanted to give you this idea."

Their response was "Honestly, David, we've just been looking at homes because we thought that's what we had to do. But buying a house right now is probably not our top priority. We'd like to meet some people, learn where the post office is, know where the bank is. This is all a little scary. So yes, we want to own a home, maybe even build our forever home, but right now, we'd appreciate being able to take a step back, not think about a sale, and focus on what matters to us. This is a great idea. Thank you."

To come full circle, in that scenario, I was their friend first and the expert second, and being present to hear their hearts led me to make the right offer for what *they* needed, not *me*.

One of the biggest and worst assumptions we make is that if someone doesn't ask us for something, that means they don't need anything. We've all heard the phrase "No news is good news," but we have to also realize that no news *is* news. People don't want to burden us, or they think we don't have time or that we don't care about their issues or that their problems are not important.

In my marriage, I'll anticipate that Jessica needs a girls' night out, so I'll tell her, "Hey, how about, this Thursday night, you get together with some friends and go do something. I'm gonna take the boys to get pizza and see a movie. Or maybe you'd rather just stay home in the quiet and relax?" She didn't have to ask. I went to her.

Everyone assumes that other people understand what they're going through. Everyone assumes that other people think the same way or that they know how someone else feels in their own shoes. Everyone assumes the way they're communicating is landing the right way and that everyone else is better off. But we all need something different at different times.

In my company, if I begin to sense some conflict among people or pick up on some discouragement with a few agents, those are triggers for me to take proactive steps. Periodically, I will bring in an outside person for a team-building day. Those are great for getting everyone in the same room and on the same page, and they can offer the entire team encouragement and confidence. We always see an upswing in collaboration when we get everyone away from work, outside the comfort zone where guards can drop, where we are all reminded of our firm foundation. People have the freedom to share things like why they came to be at DHR, what they love to do in their spare time, and what's going on in their families. There's always a lot of laughing, hugging, and a few tears.

Those days are investments in my team that come out of anticipating what they need without me asking. It's the equivalent of regular oil changes in your car. You commit to routine maintenance so you avoid a breakdown later. Aside from checking in regularly with the entire team, I also work to give each one personal time once a month to talk over anything they need from me.

4. Against Your Idols

Back when I was starting up satellite offices all over the country and speaking at big conferences, the numbers I was putting up placed my company at the top of the national rankings. I was receiving awards and a lot of attention in the media. Here's the problem with any sort of "fame," for lack of a better word: the energy and the accolades get addictive. No matter how much you receive, you want more. You need the train to keep rolling.

During that season, when I would walk into the office, my team didn't drop everything and start applauding or gather around me to listen to my tales from the road. In fact, because of my frequent absence, some relationships were even a bit strained. When I walked in the door at home after a weekend of people clamoring to ask me questions or take a picture with me, Jessica would start telling me something that happened to the house while I was away or how I needed to talk to one of the boys because of his misbehavior. The world out there at the conventions and the conferences wasn't the real world. The real world *was* back home in my office and at my house.

So the temptation is to want to get back out there where "everybody knows your name." I think this is exactly why so many celebrities and artists struggle with maintaining a family and a "normal life." The bottom line is God didn't make us to be famous. We humans just don't handle that level of attention well.

At least for me, the story I shared previously about that day after church when Jessica delivered the wake-up call for me to stop expanding my business and I saw the light, God began to show me I had created a few idols that I needed to smash and walk away from.

Now, of course, the word *idols* is understood as a biblical term, but we also use it in conjunction with people whom we admire for their talent, as in *American Idol.* But, as a Christ follower, the connotation of an idol is anything that can replace God. If you don't follow that line of belief, which is fine, then let's define an idol as anything that distracts you from your actual priorities. Was my massive expansion good for my business and my family? Ultimately, no. On paper, the numbers looked amazing. But the reality was that the entire experience was eroding everything else in my life. As soon as I stopped and got things back in the proper balance and perspective, everything got better, eventually leading to my family and my business being stronger and healthier than ever.

Back when I flirted with national expansion, the right thing for me was to shut down those offices outside Charlotte. The right thing was to get smaller. The right thing was to say no to the conferences. The right thing was to spend more time at home. The idols called out, "Let's go on the road, where everyone treats you like a king." God said, "Let's stay home and take good care of what I've given you." If we ever start believing our own publicity, we're headed for trouble.

The right thing is putting your family first, before *any* deal. As a husband and dad, that's job one. A few years ago, I had decided to make a more concerted effort as a husband and dad. After a couple of weeks went by, one night after the boys were asleep, I decided to bring up my above-and-beyond service to Jessica. I said, "Hey, I don't know if you noticed, but I've really been stepping up with the kids and with stuff around the house."

She didn't say a word but walked over to the pantry, pulled out a container, reached in, and pulled out a cookie. She walked over and handed it to me.

Puzzled, I asked her, "Uh, thanks, but what's this for?"

She smiled and said, "Well, it sounds like you want a medal, but I don't have one, so I thought I'd give you a cookie."

We both laughed, but I realized what I had done. I wanted recognition for something I already needed to be doing. It's my home too. They're my boys too. I have a clear role to her as her husband. Getting better at it and more committed is what I'm *supposed* to be doing. I thank

God that my wife "has my number" because she keeps me grounded and focused. She helps me keep the idols away.

In 2018 here in Charlotte, a church asked me to share about expressing Christianity in the marketplace. They wanted me to talk about sharing one's faith even if that means losing business. One of my key teaching points that I always talk about with Christian audiences is how so many people who call themselves Christians find their identity in their work, not in Christ. They focus on work above Jesus and, so often, even above their families. They keep him "in their pocket" and pull him out when it helps in the business relationships. But once the deal is done, they put Jesus away until the next time it's convenient. For true Christ followers, keeping him at the center of everything will keep your focus on the right thing and help you stay away from your idols.

5. Focus on the Good in a Person

The one decision I made that has helped me to live out this truth in all my circles was actually a deeply personal choice—when I called my father to forgive him. That was such a life-changing moment that most everything after that has been simple. As soon as I said yes to the gospel and I understood all that Jesus did to forgive me, I knew I had to forgive everyone who had hurt me. Since I've been forgiven and it's already been done for me, that's my only option. The grace that God has given me that I don't deserve, I just want to pay it forward. Who am I to say that someone doesn't deserve what I didn't deserve to receive? If God has forgiven me for my sins, why shouldn't I forgive my father? Nothing has been more beneficial in my life than obeying Christ, and forgiveness has been a huge part of that. Peace comes from giving grace, letting go, and not keeping score.

The day I decided to reach out to my dad, Jessica and I had talked and prayed. The hardest part was picking up the phone to dial his number. That was a battle. That was tough. That took days to do. But once I did and he answered, it immediately got easier.

I said, "I just want you to know that since I've come to know Christ, I've realized that Jesus died on the cross so that I could be forgiven and you could be forgiven. And so, I owe you forgiveness."

Dad responded, "About what?"

I answered, "About everything in our life, everything that I've been mad at you for, leaving my mom, for marrying someone who treated me badly, for ignoring what I went through, for not doing anything to end the abuse, and then for leaving me there. I've never fully understood it, but I forgive you. I've never been in your shoes. But now that I'm married with kids myself, I recognize that I'm not perfect, and I'm not the judge. So I just wanted you to know that. While I don't agree with your choices, I forgive you. I hope you understand, and now this burden is off me. And I hope it's off you too."

To my surprise, at least on that day, Dad was very nice. He sounded empathetic and even started to cry at one point. He said, "I know it wasn't good. I feel horrible. I don't remember a lot of that. It was a bad time of life, but, you know, I love you. I didn't mean for you to be harmed, so I'm really sorry."

I would love to tell you that we are fully restored and active in each other's lives today, but that would not be true. But at least the past has been forgiven, and we can communicate freely without the baggage being a roadblock anymore. When I decided to let go, the weight just came off my shoulders. I have no malice toward him. Now, what I want most is for him to know Jesus. I lived the Jewish life and came to the Messiah, so there's no reason why he can't. Regardless, I am so grateful that I have peace with my past.

This may sound very strange, but I can genuinely thank my dad and my stepmom because without them, I would not be the man I am today. My perspective, my work ethic, my lack of fear, all the things that could paralyze me, I'm grateful to them for the challenges that made me who I am.

Leaving the personal example, let's return to applying this principle to business. An overarching rule in business is that all others in your field are the competition. That dynamic creates a lot of me-against-you, too much unnecessary noise that gets in the way of deals and often hurts the clients. Let me offer you an example of how I combat that. It's what I teach my team to do. Regardless of your line of work, you can apply this truth.

In my business, a very common conflict that occurs between the buyer's agent and the seller's agent is a low-ball offer. When these happen, friction and defensiveness can quickly kick in. A kind of "How dare you?" comes into play. "Did your clients really think that's all the house is worth?" "Did you not see the finished basement?" "Did you not see the pool?" "Have you actually looked at the comps?"

When that happens to me, I know what I have to do. I come back to the agent, saying something like, "Okay, let's talk. Tell me more about what *your* clients want. Let's look at the terms. What can we do to make the offer more attractive?" The goal is to try to find out *why* a buyer made such a low offer. Is it really just a money play, or is there a good reason driving it? I try to look at how we can make the deal work rather than have everyone just stick to their guns and shoot one another.

Which brings me to another point in this truth: the right thing is usually *not* about money. Our team averages winning 86 percent of our bids. *Why?* Because we work hard to *not* make it all about money and focus on what can be good and positive in the deal. We find out the answer to "How can we customize this offer so it's the best one for you?"

Of course, there are times when you just can't make it work, and that's okay. Sometimes the house is not worth what the buyer is offering, or someone else will pay more than our client can for the house. If money's all that matters, the buyers just need to go with another offer. But we work hard to find creative ways to work with people.

When things don't go well, I firmly believe in *never* burning *any* bridge in *any* relationship even if the other people choose to burn theirs back to you. You never know when, down the road, you might need to walk over that bridge again for another person in another setting. For example, in my line of work, if you burn a bridge with one agent in a large agency, it's very likely you set fire to the entire relationship with all the other agents too. In extreme cases, this can become agency against agency, and everyone loses in those wars.

As Christ followers, we must always look at any person in any situation as Jesus does, no matter how he or she may act, speak, or even look. We seek to make the just (right) thing happen, not to enact judgment. Relationships over rules.

No matter what your business background may be, who trained you, what industry you are in, or what your personal worldview may be, I want to encourage you to look closely at how you deal with *everyone* in your life.

Realizing and changing some of your personal paradigms to make new choices to do the right thing, even if that means you don't win, could change far more than you might realize. Once again, let's close with Solomon's wisdom and counsel for life.

> My child, never forget the things
> I have taught you.
> Store my commands in your heart.
> If you do this, you will live many years,
> and your life will be satisfying.
> Never let loyalty and kindness leave you!
> Tie them around your neck as a reminder.
> Write them deep within your heart.
> Then you will find favor
> with both God and people,
> and you will earn a good reputation.
> (Proverbs 3:1–4)

APPLICATION EXERCISE

Write down any principles or truths from this chapter that stood out to you and that you want to apply in your own life.

Did any of my principles give you any inspiration or new ideas for your life? Write those down.

What is the most significant truth you discovered in this book? Explain.

How can you practically apply that truth? Write a plan.

If you are a Christ follower, was there anything you believe God spoke to your heart through this book? Explain.

Besides the one main truth that affected you in these pages, write down any others that you also want to work on and apply in time.

YOUR LIFE

I want to close by offering you a helpful three-year plan so you can successfully apply these principles for placing relationships over rules in your own life. Here's a tip: If you decide you want to do an Ironman Triathlon in three years, then you need to work backward on your timeline. If you do a 5K in year one and a 10K in year two, the bad news is you won't get to an Ironman by year three. You had better be swimming, biking, and running a considerable distance by year one and then more by year two. Setting goals in reasonable increments to arrive at your third-year goal is crucial.

Don't let the curse of the grandiose "someday" hurt you. Keep things simple. Don't get complicated. Lastly, from my experience, you will know that your plan is working if, as you meet your professional goals, you are *not* sacrificing your personal goals. Both should work together for a balanced and blessed life.

14

THE THREE-YEAR PLAN

The Why

I have the privilege of coaching top agents in real estate, as well as business leaders in the entrepreneurial space, all around the country. Over the years, I've learned that both human nature and culture teach us to say, "Let me tell you what I have to offer. Let me show you what I have of value." We're taught in the marketplace to know our worth and identify our value. But I realized a few years back that what I perceived to be a gain, someone else might consider a loss. Or vice versa.

In my own company, I have learned that before someone comes on board, I don't need to tell him or her what I have to offer. *Why?* Because I don't know what's valuable to that person. One wants more business. Another, a better-balanced life. Someone else, a stable income. Another wants the freedom to be done for the day by the time his or her child gets out of school. The reasons are as diverse as the people. I have discovered that you have to understand a person's goal before you offer possible solutions or value.

For example, I might tell a potential agent, "Hey, we can give you a constant stream of leads," and then the person responds, "I'm already working until eight o'clock every night. I need a break. I need balance. Not more business." What I offered didn't fit the desired opportunity. That's exactly the reason why I spend a lot of my first few weeks in the relationship learning what the person wants life to look like.

Today, in our breakneck-pace world, I see extremes. So many people tend to make rash decisions without a clear plan, while others are scared to death of change and get stuck. Both create their own unique set of problems.

Like I have shared about myself, some are grateful for any opportunity and say yes in the moment but, down the road, might regret making that decision. When I was in expansion mode with my business, I had a lot of people tell me yes simply because of the energy and excitement of the moment. As I've said, I have been and still can be guilty of that. There have been times when my offer didn't really fit a person's plan, but he or she jumped out and said yes anyway. Long-term, the arrangement wasn't sustainable and viable. I had to learn from that experience, which is how this exercise was born. I reached the point where I resolved that I would never again enter into any professional relationship without first knowing a person well enough to hear his or her plan.

The What

So you're growing in your career, or you own a business. Maybe you have too *much* business to navigate effectively, like I did at one point. You're thinking about jumping out on your own. Or you might be looking to get into something completely new. Some of the questions people ask me the most are

- How do I know when it's time to move, to jump, to act?
- How can I know if I'm ready or not?
- How do I decide that I need to stay where I am for now?

What I want to share with you next is the exercise I walk through with anyone who goes to work with me. I sit down with the person for some dedicated and focused time to discuss their goals, beginning with

- What does your life look like in three years?
- Professionally and personally, in three years, where do you want to be in all aspects of your life?

Here's my reasoning for the mechanics of the question. Envisioning *one year* from now, you will likely not have enough time to get everything done to meet your goals. A year will fly by. Envisioning your life in *five years*, especially in this fast-moving and ever-changing culture, is too far out in time. But three years, that's the sweet spot. Three years is far enough away to be able to get a lot done but not so far away that it seems like forever. You can also break down your goals and plan into three one-year segments.

So, right now, where do you stand with where you are in your life?

From there, you need to determine your goal.

You need to decide what must happen to accomplish that goal.

Once your goal is established, next, you need to evaluate the problem, as in the roadblocks and challenges.

Some examples might include the following:

- I don't have the funds to accomplish what I need to do.
- I don't have the mental or emotional bandwidth yet.
- I don't have enough time to develop something new.
- I can't possibly reach my goal from where I live now.

Next, we ask what action you will need to take to reach your goal.

With all these factors, a plan must be laid out.

After you set your three-year goal, figure out the problems, offer possible solutions, and create the plan, then

- if you can reach your goal on your own, jump out, leave, move, act, whatever is necessary;
- if you can do it where you are, stay, but if you can't, go where you can; or
- if you have a problem that you haven't addressed in your plan, you've got to fix that.

As I have walked people through this process, I've discovered one of the biggest wins is that everyone wants to be heard. They want someone to listen. Instead of saying no too soon, listen. Instead of saying yes too soon, listen. But yes or no is not really the issue. The solution is listening, caring, and encouraging. That's where the connection should start. Relationships over rules.

The How

Now that I've explained the Three-Year Plan exercise, I want to give you the opportunity and space to create your own. If you want to write this out in your own journal or notebook, go for it. But I want to encourage you, for your sake, to take the time to prayerfully and carefully take advantage of this exercise to set goals and be proactive about your future. The price you paid for this book might come back countless times if you change your life by implementing this exercise. If that happens, you didn't just buy a book, but you also invested in your future. *That's* my hope and prayer.

Your Plan

Professional

In three years, in my professional life, my goal (or goals) is to be:

The problem (or problems) I will have to overcome to reach my professional goal is:

Possible solutions to my problem to reach my professional goal are:

My three-year professional plan in three practical, proactive, one-year steps:

Year one:

Year two:

Year three:

Personal

In three years, in my personal life, my goal (or goals) is to be:

The problem (or problems) I will have to overcome to reach my personal goal is:

Possible solutions to my problem to reach my personal goals are:

My three-year personal plan in three practical, proactive, one-year steps:

Year one:

Year two:

Year three:

To connect your professional and personal plans, determine any conflicts between the two that need to be resolved:

Possible solutions for those conflicts are:

How can your professional and personal plan work together to create a synergy for success in your life?

CONCLUSION

My goal is that the principles I have shared with you in this book will inspire, encourage, and help you to be a better person, friend, spouse, parent, worker, and—if you are a Christ follower—a stronger member of the body of Christ. I hope and pray that these principles have challenged you in all the areas of *your* life and in *all* your circles of influence.

This world places so many rules on us every day, with that number growing every year. The list of "you can'ts" and "you shouldn'ts" have added a crushing weight to our lives. But relationships will always have more power than *all* of the rules. You have more than enough relationships in your life *right now* to accomplish any and everything you desire to do.

Never forget that God places people in your life for a reason. When that reality becomes your focus, then *anything* can be possible. You can leave behind a painful past and make your focus an exciting future. Today, trust that God has big plans for you, and *every* person in your life is a major part of that journey. I want to leave you with one of my favorite verses, Philippians 4:13: "For I can do everything through Christ, who gives me strength." May God bless you and keep you.

ACKNOWLEDGMENTS

I want to recognize each and every colleague at David Hoffman Realty and our family of services, as well as my clients and peers in the industry and my friends, new and old, for their support and faith in me over the years.

ENDNOTES

1 "Who We Are," Tax Foundation, accessed August 9, 2022, https://taxfoundation.org/about-us/.

2 "Jock Tax Displeases Baseball," *Washington Times*, May 16, 2003, https://www.washingtontimes.com/news/2003/may/16/20030516-122650-3780r/.

3 *White Christmas*, directed by Michael Curtiz (Los Angeles: Paramount, 1954), DVD, 120 min.

4 Kate Gibson, "Spanx Founder Rewards Workers with $10,000 and First-Class Plane Tickets," *CBS News*, last updated October 27, 2021, https://www.cbsnews.com/news/spanx-sarah-blakely-employees-gift-10k/.

5 Eliza Haverstock, "Sara Blakely Is a Billionaire (Again) after Selling a Majority of Spanx to Blackstone," *Forbes* (website), October 20, 2021, https://www.forbes.com/sites/elizahaverstock/2021/10/20/sara-blakely-is-a-billionaire-again-after-selling-a-majority-of-spanx-to-blackstone/?sh=1f75a747d5cf.

6 Wikipedia, s.v. "Free Refill," last modified April 26, 2022, https://en.wikipedia.org/wiki/Free_refill.

7 Amit Chowdhry, "Most of Your Facebook Friends Are Not Your Real Friends, Says Study," *Forbes* (website), January 30, 2016, https://www.forbes.com/sites/amitchowdhry/2016/01/30/most-facebook-friends-are-not-your-real-friends-says-study/?sh=1aeca0da5757.

ABOUT THE AUTHOR

David is the founder of David Hoffman Realty, an Inc. 5000 company, as well as Covenant First Mortgage and Beyond Title. David Hoffman Realty also has new homes and luxury divisions. David is consistently called on by local and national media for his expertise in real estate and economics. Over the years, his clients have come from all walks of life: from first-time home buyers and renters to high-profile clients, including professional sports figures, evangelists, actors, and actresses with multimillion-dollar listings.

Growing up in Valley Stream, near Queens, away from his mother, who lived alone in Staten Island and was paralyzed due to multiple sclerosis, David did not have the benefit of many relationships during his childhood. After leaving the house for college, David focused on making one friend at a time, always being present, and becoming the expert in his craft as quickly as possible, leading to his becoming a twenty-year-old economist.

David quickly became a nationally recognized economist in Washington, DC, while still an undergrad. David's work has been published in many major media outlets, including the *Wall Street Journal* and *New York Times*, with the US House and US Senate referencing his policy papers and economic modeling when making policy decisions.

At just twenty-four, David was realizing his dream of becoming a sports agent after being labeled nationally as the jock tax expert when, after the sudden passing of his mother, he decided to skip speaking at a sports and law conference to attend a multiple sclerosis walk in memory of his mother, whom David regretted not being able to say goodbye to. His friends said that David picked the walk over the talk. After putting the memory of his mom over his career, David decided to move south to Charlotte, North Carolina, sight unseen, leaving the rat race behind and getting a fresh start in real estate.

Today, David travels the United States and Canada, speaking at real estate and mortgage conferences, churches, and Christian concerts and music festivals on the value of the relationships in our lives, reminding many that God gives us all the gifts and people that we need to achieve our goals and dreams. He also coaches and mentors leaders of all walks of life on how they can be present and their very best both at home and in the community and marketplace.

David currently lives in Marvin, North Carolina, with his wife, Jessica, and two boys, Kane and Knox.